The U.S. Army STUDY GUIDE for Promotion and Soldier of the Month Boards

by
Roy A. Bowen

I'm truly a lucky man, I have many special people in my life. I have a good mother, brothers, sister, and the world's greatest uncle and family. This book is especially dedicated to my wife, Susi, and my daughter, Viktoria. Together they provide me with the love that helps me run down the highway toward success.

UNIVERSAL FORCES DYNAMICS

410 Delaware
Leavenworth, KS   66048
(913)   682-6518

ISBN: 0-9622627-3-0

Copy Right 1989
by Universal Force Dynamics
All rights reserved.
Printed in the United States

Cover Design: Joel Sundquist
Editor and Typesetting: Robert K. Spear

ABOUT THE AUTHOR

Roy A. Bowen was born in Winston-Salem, North Carolina and attended Western Carolina University. He spent five years as an Army Enlisted man, working in supply, NBC, training, and logistics.

Now, as the Army's Learning Center Coordinator in Munich, Germany, supervising three other Bavarian centers as well as his own, Roy assists soldiers in studying for promotion boards, Soldier-of-the-Month boards, and SQT tests on a daily basis. He brings a degree of understanding and knowledge to this study guide matched by very few. Roy currently resides in Augsburg, Germany with his wife, Susi, and daughter, Viktoria.

TABLE OF CONTENTS

SUBJECT AREA   PAGE

Military Justice	1
Wear and Appearance of Army Uniforms and Insignia AR 670-1	12
Survival, Escape, and Evasion	18
First Aid for Soldiers	21
Map Reading	32
Military Leadership	38
Flags	46
Rifle, M16A1, 5.56 MM	49
Military Customs and Courtesies	55
Origin of the Hand Salute	58
Position of Honor	62
Military Courtesy	63
Other Courtesies to Individuals	64
Uncovering	65
Actions where an Officer Enters a Facility or Vehicle	65
Meaning of the Hand Salute	66
Whom to Salute	67
When to Salute	67
Saluting in Vehicles	68
Saluting in Groups	68
The Army Song	69
Retreat	69
Salute to the Colors	70
General Orders	70
Awards AR 672-5-1	71
Duty Rosters	76
Military Sanitation	78
Army Emergency Relief	80
General Questions	82
The Army Maintenance Management System	89
Command and Other Channels	93
Equal Opportunity	94
Military Programs	99
Earning Promotion Points through Education	104
The Flag of the United States	105
Code of Conduct	106
Enlisted Promotion	109

Reenlistment	113
NonCommissioned Officers Evaluation System	117
Alchohol and Drug Abuse Prevention and Control Program	122
Nuclear, Biological, and Chemical Warfare	128
Drill and Ceremonies *FM 22-5*	136

Military Justice

1. Q: WHO MAY IMPOSE NON-JUDICIAL PUNISHMENT?
A: Any commissioned or warrant officer who holds the title of commanding officer.

2. Q: WHY WOULD A COMMANDING OFFICER SUSPEND ALL OR PART OF THE PUNISHMENT IMPOSED UNDER ARTICLE 15, FOR A SPECIFIED PERIOD OF TIME?
A: To grant a probationary period during which a service member may show that he is deserving of remission of the suspended portion of the punishment.

3. Q: WHAT IS A REPRIMAND?
A: A reprimand is an act of formal censure which reproves or rebukes the offender for his/her

4. Q: A FIELD GRADE COMMANDER CAN IMPOSE UP TO 30 DAYS CORRECTIONAL CUSTODY UNDER PROVISIONS OF ARTICLE 15. WHO MUST APPROVE THE IMPOSITION OF THAT PUNISHMENT?
A: General Court-martial Authority.

5. Q: AN ARTICLE 15 PROCEDURE BEGINS WITH THE COMMANDER ADVISING THE ACCUSED OF THE SPECIFIC CHARGE AND OR HIS/HER SEVERAL RIGHTS. NAME AT LEAST FOUR OF THESE RIGHTS.
A: Article 31 rights against self-incrimination
Consultation with an attorney
Having a spokesperson present case
Present matters in defense, mitigation and extenuation
Demand trial by Court-martial
Request an open hearing

6. Q: WHAT DOES ADMONITION MEAN?
A: It is a warning, reminder, or reproof given to deter repetition by the offender

of the type of misconduct which resulted in the admonition and to advise him/her of the consequences in the event of recurrence of that misconduct.

7. Q: WHO IS EXEMPT FROM CORRECTIONAL CUSTODY AND CONFINEMENT ON BREAD AND WATER?
A: Pay grade E-4 and above and female enlisted personnel.

8. Q: A STAFF SERGEANT TELLS YOU THAT HIS COMMANDER HAS OFFERED HIM AN ARTICLE 15. HE ALSO TELLS YOU THAT THE COMMANDER STATED THAT HIS PUNISHMENT, IF HE ACCEPTS, WILL BE 14 DAYS EXTRA DUTY CLEANING ALL THE LATRINES IN THE BARRACKS. WHAT ARE TWO ERRORS MADE BY THE COMMANDER IN THIS CASE?
A: The commander should not announce planned punishment prior to the decision to accept the Article 15. Additionally, the extra duty as stated above is not appropriate to the rank of the individual.

9. Q: CAN PUNISHMENT UNDER ARTICLE 15 BE IMPOSED WHILE A DEMAND FOR TRIAL IS IN EFFECT?
A: No.

10. Q: WHO MAY ACT ON AN APPEAL UNDER ARTICLE 15?
A: The court martial authority next superior to the officer who imposed the punishment.

11. Q: WHAT IS MITIGATION?
A: Mitigation is a reduction in either quantity or quality of a punishment, its general nature remaining the same.

12. Q: HOW DO YOU DEFINE REMISSION?
A: The action whereby any portion of the unexecuted punishment is canceled.

13. Q: MUST AN OFFICER HAVE A WRITTEN ORDER TO ARREST A SOLDIER?
A: No- The officer need only to notify the soldier that (s)he is ordered into arrest and inform him/her of the limits of the arrest.

14. Q: DOES AN INDIVIDUAL HAVE THE RIGHT TO CONTACT A LAWYER AND RECEIVE LEGAL ADVICE PRIOR TO DECIDING WHETHER TO ACCEPT PUNISHMENT OF ARTICLE 15?
A: Yes.

15. Q: WHAT GRADES CAN A COMMANDING OFFICER REDUCE UNDER ARTICLE 15?
A: Only grades that (s)he is authorized to promote.

16. Q: WHAT DOES APPREHENSION MEAN?
A: The taking into custody of a person.

17. Q: WHAT ARE THE TYPES OF COURTS-MARTIALS FOUND IN THE US ARMY?
A: Summary, Special, and General.

18. Q: CAN A NONCOMMISSIONED OFFICER BE REDUCED TO A SPECIALIST GRADE UNDER ARTICLE 15?
A: Yes- Can be reduced to a specialist rank of lower grade provided the latter grade is authorized in the PMOS of the individual.

19. Q: CAN A CIVILIAN LAWYER DEFEND AN ACCUSED IN A COURT MARTIAL?
A: Yes- Provided the lawyer meets the requirements specified in current Army regulations and the UCMJ and is paid by the accused.

20. Q: CAN A NONCOMMISSIONED OFFICER ADMINISTER AN ARTICLE 15 TO AN ENLISTED SOLDIER?
A: No.

21. Q: A COMPANY GRADE COMMANDER MAY REDUCE AN E-4 TO WHAT GRADE?
A: E-3 (One grade).

22. Q: WHAT TITLE IS GIVEN TO THE MILITARY EQUIVALENT OF THE PROSECUTING ATTORNEY IN A CIVIL COURT?
A: Trial Counsel.

23. Q: WHAT DUTIES CAN AN OFFICER ON ARREST IN QUARTERS BE ALLOWED TO PERFORM?
A: Any military duty not involving the exercise of command. If a commissioned or warrant officer on arrest in quarters is placed on duty involving the exercise of command by an authority having knowledge of the status of arrest in quarters, that status is thereby terminated.

24. Q: CAN AN ENLISTED SOLDIER BE A MEMBER OF A COURT-MARTIAL BOARD?
A: Yes- If requested in writing by the accused. The enlisted member serving on the court-martial board cannot be assigned to the same unit as the accused.

25. Q: DO YOU, AS THE ACCUSED, HAVE THE RIGHT TO BE REPRESENTED BY A MILITARY ATTORNEY OF YOUR CHOICE?
A: Yes- If the attorney has been determined to be reasonably available.

26. Q: CAN YOU REFUSE A COURT-MARTIAL?
A: Yes- You can refuse a Summary court-martial, but not a Special or General court martial.

27. Q: WHAT IS THE NECESSARY NUMBER OF BOARD MEMBERS TO CONVENE A SPECIAL COURT-MARTIAL?
A: A Special court-martial must consist of at least three members.

28. Q: WHAT ARTICLE OF THE UCMJ GOVERNS THE STATEMENTS YOU MAY MAKE ON YOUR BEHALF, YET THE STATEMENTS MAY BE USED AGAINST YOU?
A: Article 31.

29. Q: DURING PEACETIME, TO WHAT RANK MAY A COMMISSIONED OFFICER BE REDUCED BY A GENERAL COURT-MARTIAL?
A: A commissioned officer may only be dismissed from the service by a General court-martial, not reduced in rank. (During wartime a commissioned officer may be reduced.)

30. Q: HOW IS VOTING DONE ON A SPECIAL COURT-MARTIAL?
A: By secret written ballot.

31. Q: THERE ARE NORMALLY FOUR STEPS THAT ARE ACCOMPLISHED BEFORE ACTION ON AN ARTICLE 15 IS COMPLETED. WHAT ARE THE FOUR STEPS?
A: Charge
   Submission of matters of extenuation or mitigation
   Administration of punishment
   Appeal

32. Q: WHAT DOES SETTING ASIDE AND RESTORATION MEAN?
A: This is an action whereby the punishment or any part or amount thereof, whether executed or unexecuted, is set aside, and any property, privileges, or rights affected by the portion of the punishment set aside is restored.

33. Q: CAN YOU, AS THE ACCUSED, WHILE A MEMBER OF THE ARMY, HAVE AN OFFICER FROM ANOTHER MILITARY SERVICE AS YOUR COUNSEL?
A: Yes- You may be appointed any qualified officer regardless of the Armed Force of which that officer is a member.

34. Q: UNDER A GENERAL COURT-MARTIAL, AN E-7 IS FOUND GUILTY AND SENTENCED TO HARD LABOR WITHOUT CONFINEMENT. WOULD THERE BE A CORRESPONDING REDUCTION IN RANK PRESCRIBED?
A: Yes- A sentence of this type requires an automatic reduction in rank to pay grade E-1.

35. Q: ACCORDING TO THE MANUAL FOR COURTS-MARTIAL, WHAT IS THE DIFFERENCE BETWEEN ARREST AND CONFINEMENT?
A: Arrest is the restraint of a person by an order directing him/her to remain

within certain specified limits; confinement is the physical restraint of a person.

36. Q: WHAT IS THE ALTERNATIVE TO AN ARTICLE 15?
A: A request for courts-martial.

37. Q: WHEN PUNISHMENT IS ADMINISTERED UNDER ARTICLE 15, ON WHAT DATE DOES THE PUNISHMENT BECOME EFFECTIVE?
A: On the date punishment is imposed, unless otherwise prescribed by the officer imposing the punishment.

38. Q: WHAT FOUR TYPES OF PUNISHMENT CAN A COMPANY COMMANDER IMPOSE ON AN E-4 UNDER ARTICLE 15?
A: Extra duty
Reduction in grade
Restriction
Forfeiture or detention of pay

39. Q: WHO CAN IMPOSE CORRECTIONAL CUSTODY?
A: Correctional custody may be imposed only by an officer exercising General courts-martial jurisdiction, a general officer in command, or by a subordinate commander who has been granted this authority by an officer exercising General courts-martial jurisdiction.

40. Q: WHAT IS THE HIGHEST MILITARY COURT TO WHICH APPEALS ARE MADE?
A: The court of military appeals. (This court is comprised of three judges and has the final authority in cases of law involving courts-martial.)

41. Q: WHAT ACTION MAY YOU TAKE IF YOU ARE BEING TRIED BY A SPECIAL COURTS-MARTIAL BOARD AND YOU DISAPPROVE OF ONE OF THE BOARD MEMBERS?
A: You may challenge this individual and have him removed.

42. Q: WHO MAY CHANGE SPECIFIED LIMITS OF RESTRICTION ONCE ARTICLE 15 HAS BEEN IMPOSED?
A: The commanding officer who imposed the punishment, his successor in command and a superior authority.

43. Q: IF AN INDIVIDUAL IS GIVEN EXTRA DUTY AND/OR RESTRICTION UNDER THE PROVISIONS OF ARTICLE 15 AND THEN APPEALS THE PUNISHMENT, WHEN DOES THE RESTRICTION AND EXTRA DUTY START?
A: The restriction and extra duty are stayed (do not take effect) until completion of the appeal.

44. Q: WHAT IS SUSPENSION AS DEFINED BY THE MANUAL FOR COURTS-MARTIAL?

A: The action taken to grant a deserving member a probational period during which (s)he may show that (s)he is deserving of remission of the suspended portion of the non-judicial punishment imposed.

45. Q: WHAT IS THE TIME LIMIT IN WHICH AN APPEAL MAY BE MADE?
A: AR 27-10 states that appeals must be made within a reasonable time under normal circumstances not later than 15 days after the punishment was imposed.

47. Q: A GENERAL COURTS-MARTIAL MUST CONSIST OF A MILITARY JUDGE AND HOW MANY MEMBERS?
A: A General courts-martial will consist of at least five members, unless the accused requests trial by judge alone.

48. Q: WHEN AN INDIVIDUAL REQUESTS THAT ENLISTED PERSONNEL BE INCLUDED AT HIS COURTS-MARTIAL, WHAT PORTION OF THE COURTS-MARTIAL BOARD MUST BE ENLISTED?
A: When requested by the enlisted accused, at least one-third of the board must be composed of enlisted persons, unless the convening authorities directed that the trial proceed in the absence of enlisted members.

49. Q: CAN A COMMANDING OFFICER IMPOSE NON-JUDICIAL PUNISHMENT ON A MEMBER OF HIS COMMAND WHO HAS DEPARTED?
A: No.

50. Q: WHAT IS THE PURPOSE OF NON-JUDICIAL PUNISHMENT?
A: To correct, educate and reform offenders.
   To preserve an offender's record of service.
   Further military efficiency by disposing of minor infractions in a manner requiring less time and personnel than trial by courts-martial.

50. Q: WHAT IS THE BASIS FOR MILITARY LAW?
A: The Constitution of the United States: the Uniform Code of Military Justice, which is part of Title 10 of the United States Code; and the Manual for Courts-Martial, which is promulgated by Executive Order of the President.

51. Q: WHAT IS THE MILITARY EQUIVALENT TO THE FIFTH AMENDMENT OF THE CONSTITUTION?
A: Article 31, UCMJ.

52. Q: WHAT GOVERNS THE IMPOSITION OF NON-JUDICIAL PUNISHMENT?
A: Article 15, UCMJ.

53. Q: WHAT IS THE ALTERNATIVE TO ACCEPTING PUNISHMENT UNDER ARTICLE 15, UCMJ?
A: A service member may demand trial by court-martial.

54. Q: WHAT TYPES OF PUNISHMENT MAY BE IMPOSED UNDER ARTICLE 15, UCMJ?
A: Reduction, forfeiture or detention of pay, restriction and/or extra duty, written or oral reprimand or admonition.

55. Q: WHAT PERSONS MAY A COMPANY COMMANDER REDUCE UNDER ARTICLE 15, UCMJ?
A: He may reduce E-4's and below one grade.

56. Q: WHO MAY A FIELD GRADE COMMANDER REDUCE UNDER ARTICLE 15, UCMJ?
A: He may (provide he has promotion authority under AR 600-200) reduce E5's and E6's one grade. E4's and below may be reduced to Private E1.

57. Q: MAY A SENIOR NCO (E7-E9) BE REDUCED UNDER ARTICLE 15, UCMJ?
A: No, because promotion authority for those grades rests with HQDA. They may, however, be reduced for other reasons such as inefficiency.

58. Q: MAY AN NCO BE REDUCED TO A SPECIALIST RANK UNDER ARTICLE 15, UCMJ?
A: Yes, provide that the Specialist rank is authorized in his primary MOS.

59. Q: MAY AN NCO BE REQUIRED TO PERFORM EXTRA DUTY AS PART OF ARTICLE 15, UCMJ PUNISHMENT?
A: Yes, provided the duty performed is not demeaning to his rank.

60. Q: MAY AN OFFICER BE REDUCED UNDER ARTICLE 15, UCMJ?
A: No.

61. Q: WHAT RIGHTS DOES A MEMBER HAVE DURING ARTICLE 15, UCMJ PROCEEDINGS?
A: To present statements to his own behalf, or have a spokesman (not a lawyer) present and to have an open hearing.

62. Q: WHEN IS ARTICLE 15, UCMJ, PUNISHMENT EFFECTIVE?
A: Unless suspended by the officer imposing the punishment, all punishments are effective on the date imposed; however, if an appeal is made, any punishment of restriction and/or extra duty will be stayed (delayed) while action on the appeal is pending.

63. Q: TO WHOM MAY ARTICLE 15, UCMJ, PUNISHMENT BE APPEALED?
A: To the commander next superior to the one who imposed the punishment.

64. Q: MAY A COMMANDER'S AUTHORITY TO IMPOSE ARTICLE 15, UCMJ, PUNISHMENT BE DELEGATED.

A: Only an officer exercising general court-martial authority or a general officer in command may delegate his Article 15, UCMJ, authority and then only to one officer who is actually performing the duties of a deputy commander.

65. Q: WHAT IS THE MAXIMUM PUNISHMENT THAT A COMPANY COMMANDER MAY IMPOSE?
A: Reduction of one grade (E4 and below only) forfeiture of seven days pay, restriction and extra duty for 14 days, written or oral reprimand or admonition.

66. Q: WHAT IS THE MAXIMUM PUNISHMENT A FIELD GRADE OFFICER MAY IMPOSE?
A: Reduction (E5, E6- one grade; E4 and below to Private E1) forfeiture of 14 days pay per month for two months; restriction for 60 days, extra duty for 45 days or restriction and extra duty combined for not more than 45 days; and written or oral reprimand or admonition.

67. Q: WHEN DEMANDING TRIAL BY COURT-MARTIAL INSTEAD OF A ARTICLE 15, UCMJ, MAY A SERVICE MEMBER SPECIFY THE TYPE OF COURT-MARTIAL?
A: No. That is the decision of the court martial convening authority.

68. Q: MUST A COMMANDER INFORM A SOLDIER OF THE PUNISHMENT HE INTENDS TO IMPOSE WHEN OFFERING PUNISHMENT UNDER ARTICLE 15, UCMJ?
A: No, but he must inform him of the maximum punishments that may be imposed.

69. Q: WHEN IMPOSING EXTRA DUTY AS ARTICLE 15, UCMJ PUNISHMENT, MAY A COMMANDER REQUIRE A SOLDIER TO WASH AND WAX HIS POV?
A: No. The duty performed must be official and not personal in nature.

70. Q: MAY AN ARTICLE 15, UCMJ, PUNISHMENT BE CHANGED ONCE IT IS IMPOSED?
A: A punishment may be modified by the officer who imposed the punishment, his successor in command or a superior commander.

71. Q: WHAT MAY THE MODIFICATION CONSIST OF?
A: The punishment may be mitigated (reduced in nature or amount), suspended or set aside. In addition, a suspended punishment may be ordered into execution. In no case may the punishment be increased.

72. Q: MAY A COURT-MARTIAL SENTENCE A MEMBER TO BE DISCHARGED FROM THE SERVICE?
A: General and Special Courts-Martial may adjudge a discharge. A Summary Court-Martial may not.

73. Q: WHAT ARE THE TYPES OF DISCHARGES THAT MAY BE ADJUDGED?
A: A Special Court-Martial may adjudge a Bad Conduct Discharge. A General Court-Martial may adjudge either a Bad Conduct Discharge or Dishonorable Discharge.

74. Q: WHAT RIGHTS TO COUNSEL DOES A SERVICE MEMBER HAVE IN A TRIAL BY COURT-MARTIAL?
A: A member has the right to military counsel detailed by the convening authority, military counsel of his own choice (if reasonably available) or civilian counsel provided by him at no expense to the government.

75. Q: WHAT IS THE COMPOSITION OF A GENERAL COURT-MARTIAL?
A: A military judge, not less than five member plus trial and defense counsel.

76. Q: WHAT IS THE COMPOSITION OF A SPECIAL COURT-MARTIAL?
A: A military judge, not less than three members plus trial and defense counsel.

77. Q: WHAT IS THE MAXIMUM SENTENCE THAT MAY BE ADJUDGED BY A GENERAL COURT-MARTIAL?
A: A General Court-Martial may adjudge any punishment not forbidden; including where specifically authorized, the death penalty.

78. Q: WHAT IS THE MAXIMUM PUNISHMENT THAT MAY BE ADJUDGED BY A SPECIAL COURT-MARTIAL?
A: A Bad Conduct Discharge, confinement at hard labor six months, forfeiture of two-thirds pay per month for six months and reduction to Private E1.

79. Q: WHAT PUNISHMENT IS AUTOMATICALLY INCLUDED IN A SENTENCE TO DISCHARGE FROM THE SERVICE, CONFINEMENT AT HARD LABOR OR HARD LABOR WITHOUT CONFINEMENT?
A: When sentenced to any of those above a service member is automatically reduced to Private E1.

80. Q: MAY ENLISTED PERSONS SIT AS MEMBERS OF SPECIAL OR GENERAL COURTS-MARTIAL?
A: Yes, if the accused requests in writing that the court include enlisted members. They must be senior in grade to the accused and not assigned to the same unit. Enlisted persons may not sit on a court for the trial of commissioned or warrant officers.

81. Q: MAY A COMPANY COMMANDER WHO PREFERS COURT-MARTIAL CHARGES AGAINST A MEMBER OF HIS COMMAND SIT ON THE COURT THAT WILL TRY THE MEMBER?
A: No, neither the accuser or the convening authority (the officer who orders the trial) may sit on the court.

82. Q: WHAT IS THE NORMAL PLACE OF CONFINEMENT FOR A PERSON SENTENCED TO A DISCHARGE AND A LONG PERIOD OF CONFINEMENT?
A: The U.S. Army Disciplinary Barracks, Fort Leavenworth, Kansas.

83. Q: WHAT IS THE NORMAL PLACE OF CONFINEMENT FOR A PERSON SENTENCED TO A SHORT PERIOD OF CONFINEMENT WITH NO DISCHARGE?
A: The U.S. Army Retraining Brigade, Fort Riley, Kansas.

84. Q: IF YOU ARE BEING TRIED BY GENERAL COURT-MARTIAL, MAY YOUR ROOMMATE ACT AS YOUR DEFENSE COUNSEL?
A: No. Counsel before a Special or General Court-Martial must be a law school graduate, a member of the bar, and certified as competent by the Judge Advocate General of the U.S. Army.

85. Q: WHAT OPTIONS DOES AN ACCUSED HAVE AS TO THE COMPOSITION OF THE COURT THAT WILL TRY HIM?
A: He may request a panel of officers, a panel including enlisted members, he may request that he be tried by military judge alone, and he may challenge any member who he believes should not be on the court.

86. Q: WHAT IS THE HIGHEST APPELLATE COURT IN THE MILITARY SYSTEM?
A: The United States Court of Military Appeals which is composed of three civilian judges appointed by the President of the United States.

87. Q: WHEN ARE COURTS-MARTIAL SENTENCES EFFECTIVE?
A: Sentences to confinement are effective immediately. All other sentences are effective when ordered executed by the convening authority; however, a death sentence must be approved by the President of the United States.

88. Q: MAY A COURT-MARTIAL SENTENCE AN OFFICER TO BE REDUCED?
A: An officer may not be reduced during peace-time. During war-time, a General Court-Martial may sentence an officer to be reduced.

89. Q: WHAT IS REQUIRED BEFORE ANY CHARGE CAN BE REFERRED TO TRIAL BY GENERAL COURT-MARTIAL?
A: The charges must be investigated by an impartial officer appointed under the provisions of Article 32(b), UCMJ.

90. Q: MAY A MEMBER REFUSE TRIAL BY COURT-MARTIAL?
A: Only trial by Summary Court-Martial, even if he has already refused punishment under Article 15, UCMJ.

**91. Q: HOW IS VOTING DONE IN A SPECIAL OR GENERAL COURTS-MAR-

TIAL?
A: By secret written ballot.

92. Q: MAY A SERVICE MEMBER REQUEST A DISCHARGE INSTEAD OF BEING TRIED BY COURT-MARTIAL?
A: If charged with an offense which is punishable by discharge and/or confinement for six months or more, a member may request that he be discharged under Chapter 10, AR 635-200. The decision rests with the General Court-Martial convening authority.

93. Q: MAY A COURT-MARTIAL SENTENCE AN ACCUSED TO BE FLOGGED?
A: No. Flogging is a cruel and unusual punishment and is specifically prohibited by the UCMJ.

94. Q: MAY A COMMISSIONED OR WARRANT OFFICER BE SENTENCED TO CONFINEMENT AT HARD LABOR?
A: Yes, but only by a General Court-Martial.

WEAR AND APPEARANCE OF ARMY UNIFORMS AND INSIGNIA

1. Q: AR 670-1 PRESCRIBES THE UNIFORMS THAT MAY BE WORN, ITEMS WHICH MAY BE WORN ON THE UNIFORMS AND THE MANNER IN WHICH UNIFORMS ARE WORN AND THE OCCASION WHEN THE UNIFORM WILL OR WILL NOT BE WORN. TO WHOM DOES THIS REGULATION APPLY?
A: All personnel of the Active Duty Army, Army National Guard, and Army Reserve.

2. Q: WHO HAS APPROVAL AUTHORITY FOR NEW OR CHANGED UNIFORM CLOTHING AND INSIGNIA ITEMS?
A: The Chief of Staff, U.S. Army.

3. Q: WHO IS RESPONSIBLE FOR DEVELOPING POLICIES AND RECOMMENDING CHANGES FOR ARMY UNIFORM CLOTHING, ACCESSORIES AND INSIGNIA?
A: The Army Uniform Board (AUB).

4. Q: WHEN IS HEADGEAR NOT REQUIRED TO BE WORN?
A: When it would interfere with the safe operation of military vehicles, it is not required to be worn while in a privately owned or commercial vehicle.

5. Q: IF PERSONNEL ARE ON DUTY WITH TENANT UNITS ON INSTALLATIONS OF OTHER ARMED SERVICES, ARE THEY REQUIRED TO ADHERE TO UNIFORM CHANGEOVER DATES BY THE OTHER SERVICE?
A: Yes.

6. Q: WHAT ARE THE APPEARANCE STANDARDS FOR MALE PERSONNEL ON HAIRCUTS?
A: The hair on top of the head will be neatly groomed. The length and/or bulk of the hair will not be excessive nor present a ragged, unkept or extreme ap-

pearance. Hair will present a tapered appearance and, when combed, it will not fall over the ears or eyebrows nor touch the collar except for the closely cut hair at the back of the neck.

7. Q: IS THE SO CALLED "BLOCK CUT" FULLNESS ON THE BACK OF THE HEAD PERMITTED?
A: Yes, to a moderate degree.

8. Q: HOW WILL MALE SOLDIERS WEAR SIDEBURNS?
A: They will be flared, will be a clean shaven horizontal line and will not extend beyond the lowest part of the exterior ear opening.

9. Q: IF A PERSON HAS A MUSTACHE, HOW IS IT WORN?
A: It will be neatly trimmed, tapered and tidy and will not present a chopped off appearance. No portion of the mustache will cover the upper lip and not extend horizontally beyond or below the corner points of the mouth where the upper and lower lips join.

10. Q: WHAT ARE THE APPEARANCE STANDARDS FOR FEMALE PERSONNEL IN REGARDS TO HAIR LENGTH?
A: The build or length of the hair will not interfere with the wear of Army headgear. Hair will be neatly groomed and will not present an extreme, ragged, or unkept appearance. Hair will not extend below the bottom edge of the collar, nor be cut so short as to appear unfeminine.

11. Q: ARE HAIR HOLDING ORNAMENTS (BARRETTES, PINS, CLIPS) AUTHORIZED FOR WEAR BY FEMALE SOLDIERS WHILE IN UNIFORM?
A: Yes- as long as they are of a natural hair color or transparent and inconspicuously placed.

12. Q: BEFORE AN INDIVIDUAL DISPOSES OF AN UNSERVICEABLE UNIFORM, WHAT MUST BE DONE?
A: All distinctive uniform items must be removed.

13. Q: WHAT JEWELRY IS AUTHORIZED FOR WEAR WHILE IN UNIFORM?
A: A wrist watch, identification bracelet, and not more than two rings (wedding set is considered one ring).

14. Q: ARE EARRINGS AUTHORIZED FOR WEAR BY FEMALE PERSONNEL WHILE IN UNIFORM?
A: No.

15. Q: WHAT CHARGES ENLISTED PERSONNEL WITH MAINTAINING THEIR INITIAL CLOTHING ALLOWANCES, AND SUPPLEMENTAL CLOTHING ALLOWANCES?
A: AR 700-84 or CTA 50-900.

16. Q: WHAT WAS THE WEAR OUT DATE OF THE ARMY TAN SHADE 445 UNIFORM?
A: 30 September 1985.

17. Q: WHAT SHIRTS ARE AUTHORIZED FOR WEAR WITH THE MEN'S ARMY GREEN UNIFORM?
A: Army green shade 415.

18. Q: WHEN IS THE ARMY BLUE MEN'S UNIFORM AUTHORIZED FOR WEAR BY ENLISTED PERSONNEL?
A: On duty; when authorized by the local commander and off duty when appropriate.

19. Q: WHEN ARE FIELD AND UTILITY UNIFORMS AUTHORIZED FOR WEAR?
A: All year round by all officers and enlisted personnel.

20. Q: HOW MANY BELT BUCKLES ARE AUTHORIZED FOR WEAR?
A: Two: The plain-faced solid brass buckle and the black, open-faced buckle.

21. Q: WHAT COLOR WILL SHOE LACES BE?
A: Laces will be the same color as the shoe or boot.

22. Q: WHAT WAS THE WEAR OUT DATE FOR THE ARMY GREEN RAINCOAT?
A: 30 September 1985.

23. Q: ARE PATENT LEATHER SHOES AUTHORIZED FOR WEAR WITH THE UNIFORM?
A: No. Only leather or porous material is authorized.

24. Q: WHEN WORN WITH THE UNIFORM, HOW WILL THE WINDBREAKER BE WORN?
A: It will be zippered at least three-fourths of the way up.

25. Q: GIVE A GENERAL DESCRIPTION OF THE ARMY GREEN SHADE 388, SKIRT.
A: The skirt is a six-panel, knee length, slightly flared skirt, with a waistband and zipper closure on the left side.

26. Q: THE ARMY GREEN CLASSIC UNIFORM IS AUTHORIZED FOR YEAR-ROUND WEAR BY ALL FEMALE PERSONNEL. WHAT IS THE COMPOSITION OF THIS UNIFORM?
A: The classic uniform is comprised of an Army green coat, skirt, and slacks and a green shade 415 long and short-sleeve shirt.

27. Q: WHEN ARE FIELD AND UTILITY UNIFORMS WORN BY FEMALE OFFICERS AND ENLISTED PERSONNEL ON DUTY?
A: As prescribed by local commanders.

28. Q: THE HOSPITAL DUTY UNIFORM IS AUTHORIZED FOR YEAR ROUND WEAR BY ALL FEMALE OFFICERS IN THE ARMY MEDICAL DEPARTMENT. WHEN ARE ENLISTED WOMEN AUTHORIZED TO WEAR THE HOSPITAL DUTY UNIFORM?
A: When they hold a medical, dental or veterinary MOS.

29. Q: WHAT IS THE COMPOSITION OF THE MATERNITY UNIFORM?
A: The maternity uniform is comprised of an Army green shade 434 tunic, skirt, and slacks with expanded front panels, with either a white short-sleeve or Army green shade 415 long or short sleeve shirt.

30. Q: WHEN WILL THE MATERNITY UNIFORM BE WORN AS A DUTY UNIFORM ONLY?
A: Normally after the 24th week of pregnancy. Commanders may direct an individual soldier to begin wear of the maternity uniform earlier than the 24th week if the woman's condition becomes obvious in a normally fitted uniform.

31. Q: CAN A WOMAN WEAR MAKE-UP IN UNIFORM?
A: Yes, but it must be conservative and complement the uniform.

32. Q: WHAT ENLISTED GRADE IS AUTHORIZED TO WEAR THE BRANCH INSIGNIA WITH THE CLASS "A" UNIFORM?
A: Command Sergeant Major only.

33. Q: WHO APPROVES DISTINCTIVE UNIT INSIGNIA?
A: The Institute of Heraldry, U.S. Army.

34. Q: WHAT ARE BRASSARDS USED FOR?
A: Brassards are used as an identification media to designate personnel who may be required to perform a special task or to deal with the public.

35. Q: WHAT IS AN AWARD?
A: An all inclusive term covering any decoration, medal, badge, ribbon, or appurtenance bestowed on an individual or unit.

36. Q: CAN THE LONG SLEEVE GRAY-GREEN SHIRT BE WORN WITHOUT A NECKTIE?
A: No, the long sleeve gray-green shirt must always be worn with the black, four-in-hand necktie.

37. Q: WHO IS AUTHORIZED TO WEAR A PATCH ON THE RIGHT SLEEVE OF THE UNIFORM?
A: Individuals who served overseas with the units indicated by the patch dur-

ing wartime.

38. Q: CAN BADGES, RIBBONS OR UNIT CRESTS BE WORN ON THE NEW GRAY-GREEN SHIRT?
A: Yes.

39. Q: WHAT IS THE AUTHORIZED LENGTH FOR SKIRTS OR DRESSES WHICH ARE PART OF THE FEMALE UNIFORMS.
A: Not more than one inch above or two inches below the mid-knee.

40. Q: WHEN WEARING MORE THAN ONE ROW OF SERVICE RIBBONS ON THE CLASS "A" UNIFORM, WHAT IS THE DIFFERENCE BETWEEN ROWS?
A: Normally without space between rows, a space of 1/8 inch between rows may be optionally worn.

41. Q: THE ARMY BLUE UNIFORM, WHEN WORN, MAY BE CLASSIFIED AS EITHER FORMAL OR INFORMAL, WHEN IS IT CLASSIFIED AS AN INFORMAL UNIFORM?
A: When worn with a black four-in-hand necktie.

42. Q: WHAT IS THE SLEEVE LENGTH OF UNIFORM COATS AND JACKETS FOR MALE AND FEMALE PERSONNEL?
A: The authorized sleeve length for male and female personnel is one inch below the bottom of the wristbone.

43. Q: WHAT IS THE CORRECT PLACEMENT OF THE NAMEPLATE FOR MALE PERSONNEL?
A: The nameplate will be worn on the flap of the right breast pocket, centered between the top of the button and the top of the pocket.

44. Q: WHERE ARE THE SERVICE STRIPES WORN ON THE ARMY GREEN UNIFORM COAT FOR MALE ENLISTED PERSONNEL OR FEMALE GREEN PANTSUIT?
A: Four inches from the bottom of, and centered on the left sleeve.

45. Q: WHAT ENLISTED GRADE IS AUTHORIZED TO WEAR THE BRANCH IMMATERIAL INSIGNIA WITH THE ARMY GREEN UNIFORM?
A: Command Sergeant Major only.

46. Q: HOW DO OFFICERS WEAR THE INSIGNIA OF GRADE ON THE GRAY-GREEN SHIRTS?
A: On the shirt shoulder loops using the new green cloth shoulder marks.

47. Q: SERVICE STRIPES ARE WORN BY ENLISTED PERSONNEL. ONE STRIPE REPRESENTS HOW MANY YEARS OF SERVICE?
A: Three years service.

48. Q: WITH WHICH UNIFORMS ARE ENLISTED WOMEN NOT REQUIRED TO WEAR HEADGEAR?
A: With the Army mess of evening dress uniforms.

49. Q: MAY THE ARMY GREEN UNIFORM FOR MALE PERSONNEL BE WORN WITH A WHITE SHIRT AND IF SO, WHEN?
A: Yes. A white shirt with a black bow tie may be worn at formal social functions. Also, a white shirt with a four-in-hand tie during daylight social functions.

50. Q: CAN THE ARMY GREEN SWEATER BE WORN BY MALE PERSONNEL?
A: No.

51. Q: WITH RESPECT TO THE LENGTH OF THE SKIRT WORN BY FEMALE SOLDIERS, WHAT IS THE PROPER LENGTH OF EITHER THE OVERCOAT OR RAINCOAT?
A: One inch longer than the skirt.

52. Q: WHAT ARMY REGULATION PRESCRIBES THE WEAR OF THE UNIFORM BY BOTH MALE AND FEMALE PERSONNEL?
A: AR 670-1

53. Q: CAN BOTH THE SHORT AND LONG SLEEVE GRAY-GREEN SHIRTS BE WORN AS AN OUTER GARMENT WITH THE ARMY GREEN UNIFORM TROUSERS?
A: Yes.

54. Q: WHERE ARE THE SERVICE STRIPES WORN ON THE ARMY GREEN UNIFORM COAT FOR MALE ENLISTED PERSONNEL OR FEMALE GREEN PANTSUIT?
A: Four inches from the bottom of the left sleeve and centered.

55. Q: IS THE BLACK NECKTIE REQUIRED TO BE WORN WITH THE SHORT SLEEVED SHIRT WHEN WORN AS AN OUTER GARMENT?
A: No. The black necktie is not required when the shirt is worn as an outer garment but may be worn with a necktie if desired. It must however, be worn with the black necktie when the Army green uniform coat is worn.

56. Q: HOW WOULD ENLISTED PERSONNEL WEAR THE INSIGNIA OF GRADE ON THE NEW GRAY-GREEN SHIRT?
A: Enlisted personnel in the rank of Specialist and below will wear the polished pin-on insignia of grade centered on both collars with the center line of the insignia bisecting the points of the collar. They will be pinned on so the base of the insignia is one inch from the collar point. Corporals and above will wear the black and gold chevrons on their eppaulets.

17

57. Q: ARE YOU AUTHORIZED TO WEAR THE WINDBREAKER WHEN WEARING THE GRAY-GREEN SHIRT AS AN OUTER GARMENT?
A: No. This type of alteration is unauthorized.

58. Q: WHICH TIPPED BELT WOULD YOU WEAR WITH THE BLACK, OPEN FACED BUCKLE?
A: Only the black tipped belt.

Survival, Escape, and Evasion

1. Q: WHAT IS THE MOST IMPORTANT AID TO SURVIVAL?
A: The will to survive and to resist.

2. Q: WHAT FIVE RULES MUST YOU REMEMBER IN ORDER TO MAINTAIN YOUR HEALTH IN A SURVIVAL SITUATION?
A: Keep clean.
Guard against intestinal sickness.
Guard against heat injury.
Guard against cold injury.
Take care of your feet.

3. Q: WHAT IS YOUR GREATEST NEED IN A SURVIVAL SITUATION?
A: Water.

4. Q: WHAT ARE THE TWO TYPES OF EVASION?
A: Long range.
Short range.

5. Q: WHAT IS A "BLOOD CHIT"?
A: A small rayon American flag bearing an inscription in several languages that identifies the bearer as a member of the U.S. Military Forces and promises a reward for that person's return to U.S. control.

6. Q: AS AN EVADER, SHOULD YOU EVER ATTEMPT TO DISGUISE YOURSELF IN CIVILIAN ATTIRE?
A: Yes.- but only if you maintain in your possession some type of military identification such as dog tags or ID card.

7. Q: HOW MUCH WATER DOES THE BODY REQUIRE- EVEN IN COLD

WEATHER?
A: At least two quarts per day.

8. Q: CAN YOU TELL A POISONOUS SNAKE FROM A HARMLESS ONE BY THE SHAPE OF ITS HEAD?
A: No. Not all poisonous snakes have triangular or lance head shapes.

9. Q: WHAT THREE METHODS DOES AN ENEMY USE TO INDOCTRINATE YOU WHILE YOU ARE A PRISONER?
A: Repetition.
   Harassment.
   Humiliation.

10. Q: WHAT ARE THE ADVANTAGES OF EARLY ESCAPE?
A: Closer to friendly lines.
   Better directional orientation.
   Knowledge of friendly forces location.
   Better physical condition.
   Your guards not trained prison guards.

11. Q: WOULD YOU, IF EVER, DRINK POLLUTED WATER? (IF SO, UNDER WHAT CONDITIONS?)
A: Yes. However, only if you boil it then add charcoal from a fire and let it stand for about 45 minutes.

12. Q: WHEN YOU BECOME SEPARATED FROM YOUR UNIT IN ENEMY TERRITORY, WHAT ARE YOUR THREE MAJOR PROBLEMS?
A: Avoiding capture.
   Living in the field with limited equipment.
   Getting back to friendly forces.

13. Q: WHAT IS BRAINWASHING?
A: Brain washing is a calculated attempt to distort an individual's convictions and principles by means of a well planned educational process.

14. Q: WHAT DIRECTION STAR GROUP WOULD YOU USE AT NIGHT TO TRAVEL IF ISOLATED IN A SOUTHERN LATITUDE?
A: Southern cross.

15. Q: OFFICERS AND ENLISTED MEMBERS ARE SEGREGATED IN PRISONER OF WAR CAMPS. WHAT IS THE REASON?
A: To prevent their organizing.

16. Q: WHEN CAPTURED, WHEN SHOULD YOU ATTEMPT TO ESCAPE?
A: As soon as possible after capture.

17. Q: WHAT IS SURVIVAL?

A: Survival is living through a period of hardship while evading capture or while prisoner of war.

18. Q: WHAT IS EVASION?
A: Evasion is the action taken while separated from your unit to avoid capture and rejoin your unit or friendly forces.

19. Q: WHAT SURVIVAL TIPS ARE KEYED TO THE INDIVIDUAL LETTERS OF THE WORD "SURVIVAL"?
A: **S**ize up the situation.
   Undue haste makes waste.
   Remember where you are.
   Vanquish fear and panic.
   Improvise.
   Value living.
   Act like the natives.
   Learn basic skills.

20. Q: WHAT DIRECTIONAL STAR WOULD YOU USE TO TRAVEL AT NIGHT IF ISOLATED IN A NORTHERN LATITUDE?
A: Northern star.

21. Q: IF YOU ARE RECAPTURED AFTER AN ESCAPE ATTEMPT DURING WHICH A GUARD IS KILLED- CAN YOU BE PROSECUTED FOR MURDER?
A: Yes. In accordance with international law you, as an escapee, are considered to be under that country's jurisdiction and subject to their laws.

22. Q: WHAT IS A GOOD WAY TO PERSUADE YOUR CAPTORS TO ALLOW YOU TO TAKE A BATH AND WASH YOUR CLOTHES.
A: Tell your guards that you have lice. Whether it is true or not, their fear of an outbreak of louse born diseases among the civilians may prompt them to allow it.

23. Q: WHILE BEING INTERROGATED, SHOULD YOU LOOK DIRECTLY INTO YOUR ENEMY'S EYES IN ORDER TO SHOW HIM HOW TOUGH YOU ARE?
A: No. Never look directly into an interrogator's eyes. Pick a spot on his forehead and stare at it. You may otherwise answer a question and not know it.

24. Q: WHILE ATTEMPTING TO RETURN TO YOUR LINES YOU SHOULD COLLECT AS MUCH INFORMATION ABOUT THE ENEMY AS POSSIBLE. SHOULD YOU WRITE ALL THIS INTELLIGENCE INFORMATION DOWN ON PAPER?
A: No. If captured, this information could convict you as a spy. You should, however, memorize as much information as you can.

**25. Q: WHAT BASIC RULES OF TRAVEL SHOULD THE EVADER REMEM-

BER?
A: Avoid major roads.
   Avoid populated areas.
   Travel at night whenever possible.
   Take your time. Do not rush.

26. Q: WHAT IS THE FIRST REQUIREMENT FOR A SUCCESSFUL ESCAPE?
A: A well thought out plan.

First Aid for Soldiers

1. Q: WHAT FIRST AID STEPS ARE TO BE FOLLOWED WHEN TREATING HEAT STROKE?
A: Promptly immerse person in the coldest water available. If he cannot be immersed in water, get him into the shade, remove his clothing, keep his body wet by pouring water over him, and fan his wet body continuously.
Transport him to nearest medical facility at once, cooling his body on the way. If he becomes conscious, give him cool salt water to drink.

2. Q: WHAT ARE THE SYMPTOMS OF SEVERE DEHYDRATION?
A: Dizziness
   Headache
   Difficulty in breathing
   Tingling in the arms and legs
   Dry mouth
   Body turning bluish in color
   Speech indistinct
   Inability to walk

3. Q: WHAT IS FROSTBITE?
A: Frostbite is the injury of tissue from exposure to cold.

4. Q: AFTER APPLYING A PRESSURE BANDAGE TO A BLEEDING WOUND, YOU DECIDE TO APPLY A TOURNIQUET. WHERE WOULD YOU APPLY THE TOURNIQUET AND WHEN WOULD YOU LOOSEN IT?
A: Place the tourniquet 2 to 4 inches above the injury (not over the wound or fracture and preferably on a pressure point). Never loosen or remove a tourniquet once you have applied it.

5. Q: WHAT ARE THE TWO TYPES OF FRACTURES?

A: Simple- When the skin is broken, (Often called "closed")
    Compound- When the fracture protrudes through the skin surface. (Often called "open")

6. Q: HOW CAN YOU DETERMINE IF THE BLEEDING IS ARTERIAL?
A: The blood will be bright red in color and will exit the body in spurts.

7. Q: IS IT TRUE THAT PEOPLE WITH TYPE "O" BLOOD ARE UNIVERSAL DONORS- MEANING THEY MAY GIVE BLOOD TO ANYONE?
A: Yes.

8. Q: IS IT TRUE THAT THE RELIEF OF PAIN IS NOT IMPORTANT WHEN ATTEMPTING TO PREVENT SHOCK?
A: No.

9. Q: NERVE AGENT ANTIDOTE IS A MEDICAL AGENT USED FOR TREATING AGAINST WHAT TYPE OF GAS?
A: Nerve gas only.

10. Q: WHAT IS THE GREATEST DISEASE PREVENTER IN FIELD CONDITIONS?
A: Cleanliness.

11. Q: WHAT MEASURES SHOULD BE TAKEN BY THE INDIVIDUAL SOLDIER TO PREVENT ATHLETES FOOT?
A: Use foot powder daily.
   Change socks daily.

12. Q: NAME THREE TYPES OF BLEEDING.
A: Arterial
   Venous
   Capillary

13. Q: WHAT ARE THE SYMPTOMS OF TRENCH FOOT?
A: Numbness.
   A tingling or aching sensation.
   Cramping pain and swelling.

14. Q: WHAT IS FIRST AID?
A: The emergency care given to the sick, injured or wounded before medical treatment can be administered by medical personnel.

15. Q: HOW WOULD YOU TREAT A WHITE PHOSPHORUS BURN?
A: Submerge affected area in water, or apply a wet cloth or mud to the burn. Copper sulfate pads, if available, can be wet and put over the burn area. See a medical officer as soon as the mission permits.

16. Q: WHAT IS THE DIFFERENCE BETWEEN A TOURNIQUET AND A RESTRICTIVE BAND?
A: Restricting band slows the flow of blood. A tourniquet stops the flow of blood.

17. Q: WHAT IS PSYCHOLOGICAL FIRST AID?
A: Giving the patient confidence that all is well and (s)he will be all right.

18. Q: WHAT ARE THE THREE TYPES OF BURNS AND DESCRIBE EACH?
A: 1st Degree- reddening of the skin.
   2nd Degree- blistering of the skin.
   3rd Degree- charred flesh.

19. Q: HOW MANY SALT TABLETS WOULD YOU USE PER CANTEEN OF WATER?
A: Two.

20. Q: WHAT IS THE MOST IMPORTANT THING TO DO IN CASE OF A SERIOUS BURN?
A: Keep the burn clean and apply a dry sterile dressing.

21. Q: WHAT ARE THE STEPS IN ADMINISTERING FIRST AID TO PREVENT SHOCK?
A: Elevate the feet.
   Loosen clothing.
   Place covers over and under the casualty.

22. Q: YOU HAVE A MAN WITH A WOUNDED FOREARM. WHAT IS YOUR FIRST ACTION IN AN ATTEMPT TO STOP BLEEDING?
A: Direct pressure.

23. Q: WHEN AN INDIVIDUAL IS SUFFERING FROM SHOCK AND GETTING WORSE, WHAT INDICATORS WILL BE PRESENT?
A: Small fast breaths or gasps.
   Staring vacantly into space.
   Blotchy or bluish skin, especially around the mouth.

24. Q: IF YOU HAVE A SEVERELY BLEEDING CUT ON THE INSIDE PART OF YOUR WRIST, WHERE WOULD YOU APPLY A TOURNIQUET?
A: Directly below the elbow.

25. Q: HOW WOULD YOU TREAT FOR HEAT EXHAUSTION?
A: Lay the person down in a shaded or cool area.
   Remove outer clothing.
   Elevate the feet.
   Give cool salt water to drink if victim is conscious. Dissolve two crushed salt tablets or 1/4 teaspoon of table salt in a canteen of cool water and have

him/her drink three to five canteens full in twelve hours.

26. Q: HOW SHOULD YOU TREAT HEAT STROKE?
A: Lower the body temperature as quickly as possible and carry to a shaded area.
  Remove clothing and immerse body in cold water (with ice if possible).
  Keep entire body wet by pouring water on it and continuously fan to keep cool.
  Get medical aid.

27. Q: NAME SEVERAL ITEMS OF PERSONAL MILITARY EQUIPMENT THAT YOU MAY USE TO MAKE A SPLINT.
A: Rifle
  Bayonet
  Entrenching tool
  Tent poles
  tent pegs

28. Q: HOW DO YOU TREAT A PERSON FOR AN ABDOMINAL WOUND WITH PROTRUDING INTESTINES?
A: Dress the would with clean dry sterile bandages and treat for shock.

29. Q: WHAT IS THE BEST METHOD TO STOP THE BLEEDING OF A WOUND JUST BELOW THE KNEE?
A: The direct pressure method.

30. Q: WHAT FIRST AID STEPS SHOULD BE USED FOR FROSTBITE VICTIM?
A: Cover frostbitten part with warm hands until pain returns.
  Place frostbitten bare hands next to skin in opposite armpits.
  If feet are frostbitten seek sheltered area and place bare feet under clothing and against abdomen of another person.
  If deep frostbite is suspected, protect part from additional injury and get to medical treatment facility by fastest means possible. DO NOT attempt to thaw deep frostbite. There is less danger of walking on feet while frozen than after thawed.

31. Q: WHAT ARE THE "VITAL PROCESSES OF LIFE"?
A: Blood
  Circulation
  Respiration

32. Q: WHAT CONDITIONS ADVERSELY AFFECT THE VITAL PROCESSES?
A: Lack of oxygen.
  Bleeding.
  Shock.

Infection.

33. Q: IN WHAT POSITION SHOULD AN UNCONSCIOUS CASUALTY BE PLACED?
A: Place the casualty on his/her side or abdomen and turn the head to prevent choking.

34. Q: WHAT CAUSES HEAT EXHAUSTION?
A: Excessive loss of water and salt from body.

35. Q: WHAT CAUSES HEAT STROKE?
A: Prolonged exposure to high temperatures.

36. Q: WHAT FIRST AID MEASURE SHOULD BE TAKEN IN THE EVENT OF CARBON MONOXIDE POISONING?
A: Move the victim into fresh air and immediately administer artificial respiration.
Keep the victim quiet and transport to a medical treatment facility.

37. Q: WHAT PIECES OF EQUIPMENT ARE YOU ISSUED FOR PROTECTION AGAINST FIELD CONCENTRATIONS OF CHEMICAL AND BIOLOGICAL AGENTS?
A: Field protective mask.
Nerve Agent Antidote.
Decontamination and reimpregnation kit.

38. Q: WHAT ARE THE FIRST AID STEPS FOR ELECTRICAL SHOCK?
A: Turn off switch if nearby. (Do not, however, waste time looking for it).
Use a dry wooden pole, dry clothing, dry rope, etc., that will not conduct electricity to remove the person from the wire.
Do not touch the wire or the person with your bare hands. If you do, you may also be electrocuted.
Immediately administer artificial respiration. (Following removal of the victim from the electrical source).

39. Q: WHOSE FIRST AID KIT DO YOU USE WHEN APPLYING FIRST AID TO A CAUSALITY?
A: In all cases, use the victim's kit. You may need yours later.

40. Q: WHAT ARE THE SYMPTOMS OF HEAT STROKE?
A: Casualty stops sweating (this is an indicator of heat stroke and should be watched closely.)
Skin is dry and hot to the touch.
Body temperature becomes very high.
Casualty may have a headache, become dizzy or may become delirious and unconscious.

41. Q: WHAT ARE INDICATORS THAT AN INDIVIDUAL IS SUFFERING FROM HEAT CRAMPS?
A: Cramps in the muscles of the legs, arms and/or stomach. Individual may also vomit and be very weak.

42. Q: WHAT ARE THE FIVE "F'S" IN DISEASE CONTROL?
A: Food
   Finger
   Fluids
   Flies
   Feces

43. Q: THERE ARE NINE DIFFERENT TYPES OF CARRIES USED TO TRANSPORT THE INJURED OR WOUNDED. NAME FOUR OF THE NINE CARRIES.
A: Fireman carry
   Supporting carry
   Arms carry
   Saddleback carry
   Pack-strap carry
   Pistol belt carry
   Pistol belt drag
   Neck drag
   Cradle drop drag

44. Q: IF YOU FOUND A MAN WITH A HOLE IN THE FRONT OF HIS CHEST, WHAT WOULD BE THE FIRST THING YOU SHOULD DO?
A: Check the back for an exit wound.

45. Q: WHAT IS A FRACTURE?
A: A broken bone.

46. Q: WHEN WOULD YOU REMOVE A TOURNIQUET?
A: Never- Tourniquets should only be removed by trained medical personnel.

47. Q: WHAT ARE THE FOUR LIFE SAVING STEPS (IN ORDER OF IMPORTANCE)?
A: Clear the airway.
   Stop the bleeding.
   Protect the wound.
   Treat for shock.

48. Q: IF A TOURNIQUET MUST BE USED, HOW TIGHT SHOULD IT BE?
A: Severe bleeding- it should be just tight enough to stop arterial bleeding.
   Snake bite- it should be just tight enough to stop the flow of blood in the vessels, not the arteries.

49. Q: WHAT ARE THE FIRST AID STEPS FOR TREATMENT OF SNAKE BITE?
A: Keep the casualty quiet and do not allow him to walk or run.
 If possible, kill and keep the snake to assist medics in determining type of treatment.
 Make the individual as comfortable as possible- preferable in a sitting position.
 Apply tourniquet 2 to 4 inches above bite.
 Continue checking to insure pulse has not stopped.
 Should breathing stop, apply artificial respiration.
 Immobilize bitten limb in position below the heart.

50. Q: AFTER A TOURNIQUET HAS BEEN APPLIED, WHAT SHOULD BE ACCOMPLISHED BEFORE YOU LEAVE HIM AND CONTINUE WITH YOUR MISSION?
A: Dress and bandage the wound.
 Mark the casualty by placing a "T" on his forehead to alert others that a tourniquet has been applied.
 Mark the time (and day) the tourniquet was applied.

51. Q: WHAT ARE THE SYMPTOMS OF NERVE GAS POISING?
A: Running nose
 Difficulty in breathing with tightness of chest.
 Pinpointed pupils.
 Drooling.
 Excessive sweating.
 Nausea.
 Vomiting.
 Cramping.
 Involuntary urination and defecation.
 Jerking.
 Twitching.
 Staggering.
 Headaches.
 Confusion.
 Drowsiness.
 Coma.
 Convulsions and
 Stoppage of breathing.

52. Q: WHAT ARE THE SYMPTOMS OF BLISTER AGENT POISONING?
A: Inflammation.
 Blisters.
 Tissue destruction.

53. Q: WHAT ARE THE FIRST AID MEASURES FOR THE TREATMENT OF BLISTER AGENT POISONING?

A: If blisters form, cover them with loose sterile dressing and secure bandages.
Avoid breaking blisters.
If serious burns occur, seek medical care.
Use M13 decontamination kit.

54. Q: WHAT ARE THE SYMPTOMS OF A CHOKING AGENT?
A: Difficult breathing.
Nausea.
Vomiting.
Unusual shortage of breath.

55. Q: WHAT ARE THE FIRST AID MEASURES FOR CHOKING AGENT POISONING?
A: The protective mask provides complete protection. If symptoms occur, loosen clothing, avoid unnecessary exertion, keep warm and wait for medical aid.

56. Q: WHAT ARE THE SYMPTOMS OF BLOOD AGENT POISONING?
A: Rapid, severe interference with respiration.

57. Q: WHAT ARE THE FIRST AID MEASURES FOR BLOOD AGENT POISONING?
A: The protective mask provides the best protection.

58. Q: WHAT IS SELF AID?
A: Emergency treatment applied to oneself.

59. Q: WHAT ARE THE FOUR METHODS OF ARTIFICIAL RESPIRATION?
A: Mouth-to-mouth resuscitation method.
Mouth-to-nose method.
Chest-pressure arm-lift method.
Back-pressure arm-lift method.

60. Q: IN WHAT SITUATION WOULD YOU USE MOUTH-TO-NOSE INSTEAD OF MOUTH-TO-MOUTH METHOD OF ARTIFICIAL RESPIRATION?
A: If a person has a severe jaw fracture of mouth or his jaws are tightly closed by spasms.

61. Q: AN INDIVIDUAL HAS BEEN INVOLVED IN AN ACCIDENT RESULTING IN HAVING HIS FACE CRUSHED. WHAT METHOD OF ARTIFICIAL RESPIRATION IS TO BE USED?
A: Chest-pressure arm-lift method.

62. Q: IN A CHEMICALLY CONTAMINATED ATMOSPHERE, WHAT ALTERNATIVE METHOD OF ARTIFICIAL RESPIRATION WOULD BE USED AS A SUBSTITUTE FOR THE MASK-TO-MOUTH METHOD?
A: Back-pressure arm-lift method.

63. Q: WHAT IS THE PREFERRED METHOD FOR CONTROLLING SEVERE BLEEDING?
A: Pressure dressing.

64. Q: IS ELEVATION OF A WOUNDED LIMB A METHOD OF CONTROLLING BLEEDING?
A: Yes.

65. Q: WHEN WOULD ELEVATION OF A LIMB NOT BE USED AS A METHOD TO CONTROL BLEEDING?
A: Elevation must not be used if there is a broken bone in the injured part.

66. Q: IS THE TOURNIQUET THE PREFERRED METHOD FOR CONTROLLING BLEEDING?
A: No.

67. Q: WHEN SHOULD A TOURNIQUET BE USED?
A: A tourniquet should be used ONLY when pressure over the wounded area, pressure over the appropriate pressure pint, and elevation of the wounded part (if possible) fails to control the bleeding.

68. Q: TRUE OR FALSE. USE OF A TOURNIQUET HAS ON OCCASION BEEN ASSOCIATED WITH INJURY TO BLOOD VESSELS AND NERVES.
A: True.

69. Q: TRUE OR FALSE. IF A TOURNIQUET IS LEFT ON TOO LONG, IT CAN CAUSE THE LOSS OF AN ARM OR A LEG.
A: True.

70. Q: WHO MAY LOOSEN A TOURNIQUET ONCE IT HAS BEEN APPLIED?
A: Medical personnel only.

71. Q: WHEN IN THE FIELD, WHAT IS THE MOST WIDELY USED DRESSING?
A: The field first aid dressing with attached bandages.

72. Q: WHAT ARE THE BASIC TYPES OF BANDAGES?
A: Tailed, triangular, and cravat bandages.

73. Q: EVEN IF ONLY ONE EYE IS INJURED, WHY ARE BOTH EYES BANDAGED?
A: Since both eyes move together, any movement of the other eye could cause further damage to the injured eye.

74. Q: WHY IS A SUCKING CHEST WOUND PARTICULARLY DANGEROUS?
A: A chest wound which results in air being sucked into the chest cavity will

cause the lung on the uninjured side to collapse.

75. Q: TRUE OR FALSE. AN INSECT IN THE EAR MAY BE REMOVED SIMPLY BY ATTRACTING IT WITH A FLASHLIGHT HELD TO THE EAR?
A: True.

76. Q: TRUE OR FALSE. FOREIGN OBJECTS IN THE EAR CAN SOMETIMES BE FLUSHED OUT WITH WATER.
A: True.

77. Q: EVEN THOUGH FOREIGN OBJECTS IN THE EAR CAN SOMETIMES BE FLUSHED OUT WITH WATER, WHY WOULD YOU NOT USE THIS METHOD TO REMOVE SOMETHING SUCH AS A SEED OR A PARTICLE OF WOOD.
A: Flushing is never used with objects that will swell.

78. Q: WHAT IS THE PURPOSE OF IMMOBILIZING A FRACTURE BY SPLINTING?
A: Any part of the body which contains a fracture must be immobilized to prevent the razor sharp edges of the bone from moving and cutting tissue, blood vessels and nerves. Furthermore, immobilization greatly reduces pain and helps to prevent or control shock. In closed fractures, immobilization keeps bone fragments from causing an open wound and thus prevents contamination and possible infection.

79. Q: WHY SHOULD YOU NOT PROBE INTO THE NOSE TO REMOVE A FOREIGN OBJECT?
A: Probing into the nose will generally jam the foreign object tighter. Also, damage to the nasal passage can result.

80. Q: HOW SHOULD YOU TRY TO REMOVE A FOREIGN OBJECT FROM THE NOSE?
A: Try to remove the object by gently blowing the nose. If this fails, seek medical aid.

81. Q: WHAT IS THE PROCEDURE FOR REMOVING A FOREIGN PARTICLE (NOT GLASS OR METAL) WHICH IS BENEATH THE UPPER EYELID?
A: Grasp eyelashes of the upper lid and pull lid up and away from contact with the surface of the eyeball. Hold lid in this manner until tears flow freely. The tears will frequently flush out the particle.

82. Q: YOU HAVE TRIED, WITHOUT SUCCESS, TO REMOVE A FOREIGN PARTICLE (NOT GLASS OR METAL) FROM THE EYE BY CAUSING TEARS TO FLOW AND FLUSH OUT THE PARTICLE. WHAT OTHER TECHNIQUES WOULD YOU USE TO REMOVE THE PARTICLE FROM THE EYE?
A: Inspect the eyeball and lower lid. Gently remove object with the moistened clean corner of handkerchief.

If the object is not in lower lid, grasp eyelashes with thumb and index finger and place a match stick or small twig over lid, pull up and over stick. Examine inside of lid while the casualty looks down. Gently remove particle with clean corner of handkerchief.

83. Q: A PARTICLE OF GLASS OR METAL HAS ENTERED THE EYE. WHAT ACTION WOULD YOU TAKE?
A: Bandage both eyes and get casualty to a medical treatment facility.

84. Q: IF A CAUSTIC OR IRRITATING MATERIAL SUCH AS BATTERY ACID, AMMONIA, ETC., GETS INTO THE EYE, WHAT FIRST AID MEASURES SHOULD BE TAKEN?
A: Immediately flush with a large volume of water. Turn the head right to flush the right eye, turn the head left to flush the left eye. Turning the head will prevent the material from being washed into the other eye.

85. Q: HOW DOES HEATSTROKE OCCUR AND WHAT ARE ITS SYMPTOMS?
A: Prolonged exposure to high temperature may cause heatstroke. The first sign of heatstroke may be stoppage of sweating which causes the skin to feel hot and dry. Collapse and unconsciousness may come suddenly or may be preceded by headache, dizziness, fast pulse, nausea, vomiting, and mental confusion.

86. Q: TRUE OR FALSE? YOU CAN ALWAYS TELL THE DIFFERENCE BETWEEN HEAT EXHAUSTION AND HEATSTROKE BECAUSE HEAT EXHAUSTION COMES ON GRADUALLY WHERE HEATSTROKE COMES ON SUDDENLY.
A: False.

87. Q: TRUE OF FALSE? AS HEATSTROKE IS A MINOR MALADY, TIME IS NOT OF THE ESSENCE IN TREATING A PERSON WITH IT.
A: False.

88. Q: WHY IS TIME OF THE ESSENCE IN DEALING WITH A PERSON WITH HEATSTROKE?
A: It is necessary to work fast to save the life of a victim of heatstroke since the heat regulators of the body have been damaged and the body temperature may rise as high as 108°.

89. Q: WHAT IS TRENCH FOOT?
A: Trench foot is an injury which results from fairly long exposure of the feet to wet conditions, generally at temperatures from approximately freezing to 50°.

90. Q: TRUE OR FALSE? TRENCH FOOT CAN BE VERY SERIOUS; IT CAN LEAD TO LOSS OF TOES OR PARTS OF THE FEET.
A: True.

91. Q: WHAT IS THE FIRST AID TREATMENT FOR TRENCH FOOT?
A: Dry feet thoroughly and get medical treatment by the fastest means possible. If transportation is available, avoid walking.

92. Q: WHAT PARTS OF THE BODY ARE MOST EASILY FROSTBITTEN?
A: The cheeks, nose, ears, chin, forehead, wrists, hands and feet are the parts of the body most easily frostbitten.

93. Q: WHAT TWO TYPES OF FROSTBITE ARE THERE?
A: Skin only and deep frostbite.

94. Q: WHAT ARE THE FIRST AID MEASURES TO BE TAKEN WHEN DEEP FROSTBITE OCCURS?
A: Get to a medical treatment facility by the fastest means possible.
Protect the frostbitten part from additional injury, but do not attempt to treat or thaw in any way. Thawing in the field increases the possibility of infection, further damage, and gangrene.

95. Q: WHAT IS SNOW BLINDNESS?
A: Snow blindness is the effect which glare from an ice field or a snow field has on the eyes.

96. Q: WHAT FIRST AID TREATMENT WOULD YOU GIVE A PERSON WHO HAS DEVELOPED SNOW BLINDNESS?
A: Cover the person's eyes with a dark cloth to shut out all light, then take the individual to a medical facility at once.

Map Reading

1. Q: WHAT IS A BEARING?
A: A bearing is an angle measured east or west from a north or south base line.

2. Q: WHAT IS AN AZIMUTH?
A: A horizontal angle, measured in a clockwise manner from a north base line.

3. Q: WHAT IS THE RULE FOR READING GRID COORDINATES?
A: Read right and up.

4. Q: OF THE THREE METHODS USED TO INDICATE THE DIRECTION "NORTH" ON A MAP, NAME THE TWO MOST COMMONLY USED BY ARMY PERSONNEL.
A: Grid and Magnetic North.

5. Q: WHAT IS A GRID SYSTEM?
A: It is a system of vertical and horizontal lines forming squares used to determine locations on a map.

6. Q: WHAT IS THE OUTSIDE LINE ON THE BORDER OF THE MAP CALLED?
A: The neat line.

7. Q: WHAT COLOR IS USED TO DEPICT FRIENDLY FORCES ON A MILITARY MAP OVERLAY?
A: Blue.

8. Q: WHAT ARE THE TWO METHODS OF ORIENTING A MAP?
A: Aligning the map with prominent landmarks.
Using of a compass.

9. Q: WHAT IS THE SYMBOL NORMALLY USED TO DEPICT "TRUE NORTH" ON A DECLINATION DIAGRAM?
A: A star.

10. Q: WHAT IS DECLINATION?
A: The angular difference between true north and either magnetic or grid north.

11. Q: HOW MANY SCALES ARE THERE ON A COMPASS FACE?
A: Two- one graduated in mils and the other in degrees.

12. Q: WHAT DOES THE GRAPHIC SCALE OF MAP TELL US?
A: It provides us with a highly accurate method for measuring ground distance on a map.

13. Q: IF YOU ARE TRAVELING ON AN AZIMUTH OF 90°, WHAT DIRECTION ARE YOU TRAVELING?
A: East.

14. Q: WHAT IS A SPECIAL PURPOSE MAP?
A: A special map is one that has been designed or modified to give information not covered on a standard map or to elaborate on a standard map.

15. Q: NAME THE TWO TYPES OF GRID SYSTEMS USED BY THE MILITARY?
A: Universal Transverse Mercator (UTM)
Universal Polar Stereographic

16. Q: WHAT IS LATITUDE?
A: Latitude is the distance of a point north or south of the equator, going east or west.

17. Q: WHAT IS THE FIRST CONSIDERATION IN THE CARE OF MAPS?
A: Proper folding.

18. Q: WHAT IS MEANT BY MARGINAL DATA?
A: Data found on the margin of a map which gives details of a technical nature that must be known if the map is to be read correctly.

19. Q: IN THE ABSENCE OF COLORS, HOW DO YOU INDICATE ENEMY AND FRIENDLY POSITIONS?
A: Double line- enemy.
Single line- friendly.

20. Q: WHAT ARE THREE TYPES OF SLOPES?
A: Uniform
Concave
Convex

21. Q: IF YOU SEE A SYMBOL ON A MAP THAT YOU ARE NOT FAMILIAR WITH, HOW DO YOU DETERMINE WHAT IT IS?
A: Check the legend of the map.

22. Q: HOW MANY MILS ARE THERE IN A CIRCLE?
A: 6,400.

23. Q: DEFINE RESECTION?
A: Resection is the location of the user's unknown position by sighting on two or more known features.

24. Q: HOW MANY DEGREES DOES EACH CLICK ON THE BEZEL OF THE LENSATIC COMPASS REPRESENT?
A: Three degrees per click.

25. Q: WHAT IS AN OVERLAY?
A: A transparent or translucent medium upon which special military information has been plotted at the same scale of a map, photograph, or other graphic.

26. Q: CONTOUR LINES WILL ALWAYS CROSS A RIVER OR STREAM IN A

WAY WHICH INDICATES EITHER AN UPSTREAM OR DOWNSTREAM DIRECTION. OF THE TWO DIRECTIONS MENTIONED, WHICH IS CORRECT?
A: Upstream.

27. Q: WHAT IS THE BASIC RULE FOR COMPUTING A BACK AZIMUTH?
A: If the azimuth is more than 180 degrees, subtract 180 degrees.
If the azimuth is less than 180 degrees, add 180 degrees.

28. Q: PLACING A MAP SO THAT MAGNETIC NORTH ON THE MAP COINCIDES WITH MAGNETIC NORTH ON THE GROUND IS ONE WAY OF DOING WHAT?
A: Orienting the map.

29. Q: WHAT TWO THINGS CAN YOU USE AS A GUIDE FOR TRAVELING THROUGH AN UNKNOWN AREA IF YOU DO NOT HAVE A COMPASS?
A: Sun and stars.

30. Q: HOW MANY METERS ARE THERE IN A GRID SQUARE?
A: 1,000 meters.

31. Q: IN PREPARING AN OVERLAY OF A SPECIFIC MAP FOR COMBAT OPERATIONS, VARIOUS ABBREVIATIONS ARE USED TO INDICATE BOUNDARIES AND LIMITING POINTS. I WILL STATE THE ABBREVIATIONS AND YOU RESPOND WITH THE MEANING OF EACH.
A: FEBA- Forward Edge of the Battle Area.
MSR- Main Supply Route.
COPL- Combat Outpost Line
LD- Line of Departure
RSL- Reconnaissance and Security Line

32. Q: IN WHAT DIRECTION DOES THE ARROW ON A COMPASS ALWAYS POINT?
A: Magnetic North.

33. Q: CAN A LENSATIC COMPASS BE USED AT NIGHT?
A: Yes.

34. Q: OF THE TWO TYPES OF COMPASSES USED IN THE ARMY TODAY, WHICH TYPE IS MOST COMMON AMONG TROOP UNITS?
A: The lensatic compass.

35. Q: HOW CLOSE TO YOUR TARGET WILL A SIX DIGIT COORDINATE PUT YOU?
A: Within 100 meters.

36. Q: WHAT IS A MILITARY GRID SYSTEM?
A: A network of squares formed by vertical (north-south) and horizontal (east-

west) lines and used to locate an area or thing on a map.

37. Q: WHAT IS INTERSECTION?
A: Locating an unknown point by successively occupying two known positions and sighting on the unknown point. It is used primarily to locate features that do not appear on a map.

38. Q: SOMETIMES THE "SCALE" ON A MAP WILL BE REFERRED TO BY ANOTHER TERM. WHAT IS THAT TERM?
A: Representative fraction.

39. Q: WHAT MUST BE ACCOMPLISHED PRIOR TO PLOTTING AN AZIMUTH ON A MAP?
A: Orient oneself to the map- with the terrain or with a compass.

40. Q: THERE ARE TWO PRECAUTIONS YOU MUST TAKE WHEN USING A COMPASS WHAT ARE THEY?
A: Never take a compass reading near visible masses of metal.
Never take a compass reading near any type of electrical circuits, power lines, etc.

41. Q: WHAT DOES REPRESENTATIVE FRACTION MEAN WHEN APPLIED TO MAP READING?
A: It is the ratio of horizontal distance on a map to the corresponding horizontal distance on the ground.

42. Q: WHY ARE MAPS IMPORTANT?
A: When used correctly, a map can give accurate distances, locations, heights, best routes, key terrain features, and concealment and cover information.

43. Q: HOW CLOSE TO YOUR TARGET WILL A FOUR DIGIT GRID COORDINATE PUT YOU?
A: Within 1000 meters.

44. Q: WHAT IS RESECTION?
A: Resection is the location of the user's unknown position by sighting on two or three known features.

45. Q: HOW DO YOU OBTAIN A BACK AZIMUTH?
A: A back azimuth is the reverse direction of an azimuth. To obtain a back azimuth from an azimuth add 180°, if the azimuth is less than 180°, or subtract 180°, if the azimuth is larger than 180°.

46. Q: HOW MANY SCALES ARE THERE ON A COMPASS FACE?
A: Two- one graduated in mils and the other in degrees.

47. Q: HOW MANY MILS ARE THERE IN A CIRCLE?

A: 6400.

48. Q: IF YOU SEE A SYMBOL ON A MAP THAT YOU ARE NOT FAMILIAR WITH, HOW DO YOU FIND OUT WHAT IT IS?
A: Look in the legend of the map.

49. Q: WHICH SCALE OF A MAP WOULD COVER MORE AREA ON THE GROUND, 1:25,000 OR 1: 50,000?
A: 1:50,000. The larger the number after "1:", the smaller the scale of the map.

50. Q: WHAT ARE PROTRACTORS USED FOR?
A: Dividing a circle into units of angular measure.

51. Q: HOW ARE MAN-MADE AND NATURAL FEATURES DEPICTED ON A MAP?
A: By symbols, lines, colors and forms.

52. Q: THERE ARE 21 ITEMS WHICH MIGHT BE INCLUDED IN THE MARGINAL DATA ON A MAP, CAN YOU NAME SIX OF THEM?
A: (1) Sheet name (generally a map is named after its outstanding cultural or geographical feature)
(2) Sheet number.
(3) Series name and scale.
(4) Series number.
(5) Edition number.
(6) Bar scales (rulers used to convert map distance to ground distance.
(7) Credit note.
(8) Adjoining sheets diagram.
(9) Index to boundaries.
(10) Projection note.
(11) Grid note.
(12) Grid reference box.
(13) Vertical datum note.
(14) Horizontal datum note.
(15) Legend (explanation of symbols used.)
(16) Declination diagram.
(17) User's note.
(18) Unit imprint (the agency which printed the map and the printing date.)
(19) Contour interval.
(20) Special notes and scales.
(21) Stock number identification.

53. Q: WHAT ARE BAR SCALES AND WHERE ARE THEY LOCATED ON A MAP?
A: Bar scales are rulers used to convert map distance to ground distance and are located in the center of the lower margin.

Military Leadership

1. **Q: WHAT ARE THE TWO TYPES OF MILITARY LEADERSHIP?**
   A: Authoritarian (autocratic)
   Persuasive (democratic)

2. **Q: THERE ARE FIVE STEPS FOLLOWED IN PREPARING TO COUNSEL A SOLDIER, WHAT ARE THEY?**
   A: Advance notification.
   Selection of site.
   Schedule of a time.
   General outline.
   Create desired atmosphere.

3. **Q: HOW DO YOU DEFINE MORALE?**
   A: Morale is the state of mind of an individual.

4. **Q: WHAT IS TACT?**
   A: Tact is the ability to deal with others in a respectful manner.

5. **Q: WHAT IS MILITARY LEADERSHIP?**
   A: It is the process of influencing men/women in such a manner as to accomplish the mission.

6. **Q: WHAT IS THE ULTIMATE OBJECTIVE OF MILITARY LEADERSHIP?**
   A: The accomplishment of the mission.

7. **Q: WHAT IS PERFORMANCE COUNSELING?**
   A: The process of communicating to a subordinate the leader's assessment of the strong and weak aspects of the subordinates' performance of duty and suggesting ways in which that performance may be improved.

8. Q: NAME THE THREE PHASES OF THE DECISION MAKING PROCESS.
A: Prepare.
   Decide.
   Act.

9. Q: WHAT ARE THE TWO BASIC RESPONSIBILITIES OF A LEADER?
A: Accomplishment of the mission.
   Welfare of his men and women.

10. Q: WHAT ACTION SHOULD A SOLDIER TAKE WHEN (S)HE HAS A FAMILY PROBLEM WHICH IS AFFECTING PERFORMANCE?
A: Seek counseling or advice from the immediate supervisor.

11. Q: IN MANY INSTANCES, A COUNSELOR CANNOT HELP THE SOLDIER WITH A PROBLEM BECAUSE THE PROBLEM OBVIOUSLY REQUIRES PROFESSIONAL COUNSELING. WHEN THIS HAPPENS THE SOLDIER MUST BE REFERRED TO AN OUTSIDE AGENCY. NAME THREE SUCH AGENCIES.
A: American Red Cross.
   Army Community Service.
   Army Emergency Relief.
   Chaplain.
   Mental Hygiene
   Social Work Service.

12. Q: THERE ARE 14 TRAITS DESIRABLE OF EVERY LEADER, CAN YOU NAME SIX?

A: Bearing	Endurance
Unselfishness	Dependability
Integrity	Justice
Courage	Enthusiasm
Knowledge	Tact
Decisiveness	Loyalty
Initiative	Judgement

NOTE: Most of the above traits can be remembered by using the following words: BUICK   DIED   JET

13. Q: WHAT IS BEARING?
A: Bearing is a man's general appearance, carriage, deportment and conduct.

14. Q: WHAT IS COURAGE?
A: Courage is a mental quality that recognizes fear of danger or criticism, but enables a man to proceed in the face of it with calmness and firmness.

15. Q: WHAT IS DECISIVENESS?
A: The ability to make clear decisions promptly and to state them in a clear,

forceful manner.

16. Q: WHAT IS DEPENDABILITY?
A: The certainty of proper performance of duty.

17. Q: DEFINE ENDURANCE.
A: The mental and physical stamina measured by the ability to withstand pain, fatigue, stress and hardship.

18. Q: DEFINE ENTHUSIASM.
A: The display of sincere interest and zeal in the performance of duties.

19. Q: WHAT IS INITIATIVE?
A: Taking action in the absence of orders.

20. Q: INTEGRITY IS DEFINED AS WHAT?
A: The uprightness and soundness of mental principles, the quality of truthfulness and honesty.

21. Q: WHAT IS JUDGEMENT?
A: The ability to logically weigh facts and possible solutions on which to base sound decisions.

22. Q: IN ADDITION TO THE 14 TRAITS OF LEADERSHIP, THERE ARE 11 "PRINCIPLES" WHICH HELP US IN THE APPLICATION OF THESE TRAITS. NAME THREE OF THE 11.
A: Know yourself and seek self-improvement.
   Seek responsibility and take responsibility for your actions.
   Be technically and tactically proficient.
   Make sound and timely decisions.
   Set the example.
   Know your soldiers and look out for their welfare.
   Keep your soldiers informed.
   Develop a sense of responsibility in your subordinates.
   Insure that the task is understood, supervised and accomplished.
   Train your soldiers as a team.
   Employ your unit in accordance with its capabilities.

23. Q: EVERY MILITARY LEADER MUST BE A PROFESSIONAL. WHY IS PROFESSIONALISM IMPORTANT IN THE MILITARY?
A: There are two reasons why professionalism is important in the military: 1) The military leader is a public servant responsible for defense of the nation and 2) The military organization is often responsible for the life of its soldiers.

24. Q: THERE ARE FOUR TYPES OF COUNSELING. WHAT ARE THEY?
A: Performance counseling.
   Personal counseling.

Professional counseling.
Career counseling.

25. Q: LEADERS AT ALL LEVELS MUST USE JUSTICE WHEN EXERCISING LEADERSHIP, WHAT DOES THIS MEAN?
A: The leader must give reward and punishment according to the merit of the case in question.

26. Q: AFTER YOU HAVE COUNSELED A SOLDIER ON A SPECIFIC PROBLEM, WHAT MUST YOU AS A LEADER DO TO INSURE THAT THE PROBLEM HAS BEEN RESOLVED?
A: Follow-up.

27. Q: DEFINE "COMMAND."
A: The authority a person in the military lawfully exercises over subordinates by virtue of his rank and assignment or position.

28. Q: WHAT ARE THE INDICATORS OF LEADERSHIP?
A: Morale
Esprit De Corps
Discipline
Proficiency

29. Q: HOW DO YOU DEFINE "ESPRIT DE CORPS?"
A: Esprit De Corps is the loyalty to, pride, and enthusiasm for the unit shown by its members.

30. Q: WITHIN THE MILITARY "DISCIPLINE" HAS THREE SEPARATE MEANINGS. THE FIRST IS PUNISHMENT- WHAT ARE THE OTHER TWO AND WHICH IS CONSIDERED TO BE THE MOST CONSTRUCTIVE?
A: Obedience and Self-Control (this is the most constructive.)

31. Q: THERE ARE THREE WAYS BY WHICH A LEADER MAY PERFORM COUNSELING. WHAT ARE THEY?
A: Directive
Non-directive
Combined

32. Q: THERE ARE SEVERAL PITFALLS IN COUNSELING. ONE OF THEM IS THE "HALO EFFECT"- WHAT IS MEANT BY THIS TERM?
A: The tendency to judge a subordinate on the basis of a specific trait of behavior or appearance rather than the "whole person" concept.

33. Q: INDIVIDUALS REACT IN MANY WAYS TO COUNSELING. ONE REACTION IS THE "TOO EASY" AGREEMENT. WHEN CONFRONTED WITH THIS SITUATION WHAT SHOULD YOU DO?
A: Review the points of the discussion for reinforcement or, if deemed neces-

sary, have the counselee review them.

34. Q: A GOOD LEADER UNDERSTANDS COMPLETELY THE THREE TYPES OF APPROACHES TO COUNSELING AND SELECTS THE PROPER APPROACH BASED ON THE CIRCUMSTANCES AND INDIVIDUAL INVOLVED. "DIRECTIVE", "NON-DIRECTIVE" AND "COMBINED" ARE THE THREE APPROACHES AVAILABLE FOR USE. I'LL REPEAT ONE OF THE THREE AND I WANT YOU TO DEFINE IT FOR ME-
A: **Directive**- The counselor assumes the dominant role. It is counselor centered. He advises, offers explanations or tells the individual what alternatives are available.
Non-directive- This type is soldier-centered. The counselor causes the individual to take complete responsibly for solving the problem. The session is only partially structured by the counselor and the individual selects the topic of discussion.
Combined- A mixture of the first two. Use of this method depends on the counselors assessment of the situation.

35. Q: PART OF A LEADER'S JOB IS TO PROPERLY MOTIVATE HIS SUBORDINATES. THE FIRST THING HE MUST DO IS INSURE HIS SOLDIERS ARE AWARE OF THE FORMAL AND INFORMAL CONTRACT BETWEEN THE SOLDIER AND THE ARMY. WHAT IS MEANT BY "FORMAL" AND "INFORMAL" CONTRACT?
A: Formal- Military obligation an individual incurs when (s)he is sworn in to military service.
  Informal- Those implied obligations and responsibilities which the organization and the soldiers have to each other.

36. Q: THERE ARE SEVERAL CONDITIONS WHICH CREATE A CLIMATE OF DISCIPLINE WITHIN A UNIT. LEADERS MUST MAKE EVERY EFFORT TO FOSTER AND MAINTAIN SUCH A CLIMATE. ONE SUCH CONDITION IS "CLEARLY STATED AND ENFORCEABLE PERSONAL STANDARDS." WHAT ARE SOME OF THE OTHERS?
A: High performance standards.
  Competitive activities.
  Tough, stressful training.
  Fair and just system of rewards and punishments.
  Loyalty to supervisors and subordinates.
  Open channels of communication.
  Reduction of troop frustrations.
  Analysis of current rules and policies to update and eliminate those no longer productive.

37. Q: A GOOD LEADER MUST BE CAPABLE OF MAKING DECISIONS CONCERNING SIMPLE AS WELL AS COMPLEX SUBJECTS. THE DECISION MAKING PROCESS CONSISTS OF THREE PHASES... "PREPARE", "DECIDE" AND "ACT." THE SECOND PHASE (THE DECIDE PHASE) REQUIRES

A LEADER TO PERFORM THREE SEPARATE STEPS. THE FIRST STEP IS "DEVELOP AND LIST COURSES OF ACTION" - WHAT ARE THE OTHER TWO?
A: Analyze courses of action.
   Select best course of action.

38. Q: YOU ARE A SQUAD LEADER OR SECTION LEADER, HOW DO YOU RECOGNIZE THE NEED FOR COUNSELING IN YOUR SOLDIERS?
A: A good performer consistently begins to perform poorly.
   A normally attentive person suddenly acts disinterested.
   A soldier performs deliberate acts of misconduct or refuses to follow instructions or
   orders.
   A normally outgoing soldier becomes withdrawn and a loner.

39. Q: WHAT IS COUNSELING?
A: Counseling is a process for assisting a person to find answers to his problems.

40. Q: IS COUNSELING LIMITED TO POOR PERFORMERS?
A: No- A good performer should also be counseled in order to satisfy the need for self-esteem and motivate him/her to continue to perform well.

41. Q: WHAT IS THE OBJECTIVE OF MILITARY LEADERSHIP?
A: The successful accomplishment of the mission.

42. Q: WHAT IS COMMAND PRIMARILY BASED ON?
A: Authority delegated through the chain of command.

43. Q: WHAT MUST A COMMANDER USE TO ATTAIN THE NUMEROUS GOALS OF HIS ORGANIZATION?
A: He must use good leadership techniques in dealing with his men and women and good management techniques in organizing and providing the resources necessary to accomplish the mission.

44. Q: WHAT IS MANAGEMENT?
A: The process of planning, organizing, coordinating, directing, and controlling resources such as men, material, time and money to accomplish the organizational mission.

45. Q: WHAT DOES A COMMANDER DO WHEN HE IS UNABLE TO PERSONALLY SUPERVISE EACH ACTIVITY?
A: He delegates his authority and thereby uses his subordinates to assist him in the accomplishment of the mission.

46. Q: WHAT IS MEANT BY "A COMMANDER MUST WEAR TWO HATS?
A: It means he must be both a leader and a manager.

47. Q: WHAT ARE THE THREE ATTRIBUTES OF MILITARY PROFESSIONALISM?
A: Technical competence, values attributes and ethical conduct.

48. Q: WHAT ARE VALUES?
A: Values are attitudes for or against an event based on the belief that it helps or harms some person, group or institution.

49. Q: WHAT IS STRESS?
A: Stress is a force directed at an object.

50. Q: THE CAUSES OF FRUSTRATION CAN BE CATEGORIZED INTO TWO MAJOR TYPES; WHAT ARE THEY?
A: Delaying or blocking and conflicting causes.

51. Q: WHAT IS THE FINAL AND MOST IMPORTANT FACTOR IN MINIMIZING THE AWOL PROBLEM?
A: The leader.

52. Q: HOW CAN A LEADER ENHANCE HIS ABILITY TO COUNSEL?
A: By mastering the skills and techniques of counseling.

53. Q: WHO DEVELOPS COUNSELING SKILLS?
A: The unit commander.

54. Q: WHAT IS COUNSELING?
A: Counseling is a process of identifying the nature of the problem and applying the proper counseling techniques.

55. Q: HOW ARE COUNSELING SKILLS DEVELOPED?
A: Counseling skills are developed by studying the rudiments of human behavior, knowing the problem areas affecting subordinates and becoming proficient in dealing with counselees.

56. Q: WHAT ARE THE FIVE STEPS IN PREPARING TO COUNSEL?
A: Advance notification
   Selection of site
   Schedule of time
   General outline
   Create a desired atmosphere

57. Q: WHAT IS INVOLVED IN COMMUNICATION SKILLS?
A: Effective listening and speaking.

58. Q: WHAT IS INVOLVED IN OBSERVATION SKILLS?
A: Looking and listening.

59. Q: WHAT IS A GOOD METHOD TO USE WHEN TRYING TO OBTAIN INFORMATION DURING COUNSELING?
A: The Question Technique.

60. Q: WHAT ARE TWO BASIC TYPES OF COUNSELING FOUND IN THE MILITARY SERVICE?
A: Performance and career.

61. Q: WHAT IS PERSONAL COUNSELING?
A: The discussing of a soldier's problem in an effort to help him solve it.

62. Q: WHICH AGENCIES CAN ASSIST A LEADER WITH PROBLEMS IN WHICH HE IS NOT QUALIFIED TO ASSIST?
A: American Red Cross
Army Community Service
Army Emergency Relief
Chaplain
Inspector General
Legal Assistance
Personal Affairs
Mental Hygiene
Social Work Service

63. Q: WHAT IS THE PURPOSE OF TRAINING?
A: To prepare soldiers for job duty performance.

64. Q: WHAT IS DECISION MAKING?
A: A process for selecting a course of action for more alternatives for the purpose of achieving a desired result.

65. Q: WHAT MUST A LEADER DO FIRST TO BE AN EFFECTIVE COUNSELOR?
A: Be available for his men.

Flags

1. Q: HOW MANY U.S. FLAGS ARE AUTHORIZED TO BE FLOWN ON ANY ARMY INSTALLATION?
A: Only one, unless authorized by Headquarters, Department of the Army.

2. Q: WHEN IS A NEW STAR ADDED TO THE U.S. FLAG?
A: When a new state is admitted to the Union.

3. Q: WHAT IS THE HEIGHT OF A FLAG POLE AT A PERMANENT INSTALLATION?
A: Fifty, sixty, or seventy-five feet in height, of permanent construction.

4. Q: WHAT IS THE PROPER WAY TO LOWER THE FLAG FROM HALF STAFF?
A: It is raised to the top first and then lowered.

5. Q: HOW SHOULD THE U.S. FLAG BE DISPLAYED AGAINST A WALL?
A: Either horizontally or vertically, with the union uppermost and to the flag's own right. It will be flat and hanging free.

6. Q: AT BURIAL SERVICES, TO WHOM IS THE FLAG GIVEN?
A: It is presented to the "primary next of kin" and/or parents of the deceased.

7. Q: WHEN WILL THE POST FLAG BE HOISTED?
A: Only in pleasant weather.

8. Q: WHEN IS THE STORM FLAG FLOWN?
A: In stormy or windy weather or any weather during such hours as may be designated by the commanding officer.

9. Q: WHEN WILL THE GARRISON FLAG BE FLOWN?
A: On holidays and important occasions, when authorized.

10. Q: WHAT IS A GUIDON?
A: A company, battery, or troop identification flag.

11. Q: WHEN A NUMBER OF FLAGS ARE DISPLAYED, HOW WILL THE U.S. FLAG BE DISPLAYED?
A: The flag of the United States will be displayed at the marching right of the line, to the observer's left.

12. Q: WHAT DO THE COLORS ON THE U.S. FLAG SYMBOLIZE?
A: White- Purity and innocence.
Blue- Vigilance, perseverance and justice.
Red- Hardiness and valor.

13. Q: WHAT IS KNOW AS THE FLY OF A FLAG?
A: The length.

14. Q: WHAT IS THE HOIST OF A FLAG?
A: The width.

15. Q: WHAT ARE THE FOUR AUTHORIZED STAFFHEADS THAT CAN BE USED ON FLAGPOLES AND FLAGSTAFFS?
A: Eagle
Acorn
Ball
Spear

16. Q: WHO IS AUTHORIZED A U.S. FLAG OVER THEIR CASKET AT A MILITARY FUNERAL?
A: Any member of the military service on active duty.
Members of the National Guard.
Members of the U.S. Army Reserve
Members of recognized military organizations.
Former members of the Armed Services who have been honorably discharged

17. Q: HOW ARE THE STRIPES ARRANGED ON THE FLAG?
A: Thirteen stripes, 7 red and 6 white- starting and ending with red.

18. Q: WHAT THREE OTHER NAMES ARE USED IN MILITARY SERVICE FOR THE FLAG OF THE UNITED STATES?
A: **Color**- A flag carried by dismounted units, supreme commanders and certain general officers.
Standard- A flag carried by mounted or motorized units.
Ensign- A flag flown on ships, small boats and airships.

19. Q: WHY DOES THE ARMY HAVE A RETREAT FORMATION?

A: Retreat is a ceremony in which the units pays honor to the Untied States Flag when it is lowered in the evening.

20. Q: CAN ANY FLAG BE FLOWN ABOVE THE U.S. FLAG? IF SO, WHEN AND WHAT?
A: Only a religious flag, during religious ceremonies, while on a ship.

21. Q: WHEN THE GUIDON BEARER IS NOT IN FORMATION AND THE OCCASION ARISES WHERE HE SHOULD SALUTE AS AN INDIVIDUAL, HOW DOES HE SALUTE?
A: He executes "Present Guidon" in the same manner as present arms with a rifle.

22. Q: WHEN THE AMERICAN FLAG IS DRAPED OVER A CASKET, WHERE ARE THE STARS LOCATED?
A: Over the left shoulder of the deceased.

23. Q: HOW LONG IS THE AMERICAN FLAG FLOWN AT HALF STAFF AFTER THE DEATH OF A PRESIDENT OR FORMER PRESIDENT?
A: Thirty days.

24. Q: WHEN MILITARY PERSONNEL DIE AND THE AMERICAN FLAG IS PRESENTED TO THE FAMILY OF THE DECEASED, WHERE DOES THE FLAG COME FROM?
A: Active duty- from Branch of Service concerned.
    Retired- from the Veterans Administration.

25. Q: WHEN A PRESIDENT OF THE UNITED STATES DIES, HOW IS THE FLAG PLACED AT HALF STAFF?
A: Raise the flag to the top and then lower it to half staff. (same procedure any time the flag is to be flown at half staff.)

RIFLE, M16A1, 5.56MM

1. Q: WHAT IS THE RECOMMENDED BASIC LOAD OF AMMUNITION TO BE CARRIED BY AN INDIVIDUAL FOR THE M16A1?
A: 140 rounds. (If you count the 140 rounds to be carried by an individual and add the additional 70 rounds to be carried in a vehicle the total would be 210 rounds).

2. Q: WHAT IS THE DESCRIPTION OF AN M16A1 RIFLE?
A: It is a 5.56mm, magazine-fed, gas-operated shoulder weapon. It is designed for either semiautomatic or automatic fire through the use of a selector lever.

3. Q: WHAT IS THE BATTLESIGHT SETTING IN METERS FOR THE M16A1 RIFLE?
A: Two hundred and fifty meters.

4. Q: WHAT SHOULD YOU DO IF A NOTICEABLE DIFFERENCE IN SOUND OR RECOIL IS EXPERIENCED DURING FIRING OF THE M16A1 RIFLE?
A: Stop firing and check for a bullet in the bore.

5. Q: WHAT IS THE IMMEDIATE ACTION YOU MUST TAKE IF YOU HAVE A STOPPAGE WITH THE M16A1 RIFLE?
A: 1) Immediate action is the unhesitating application of a probable remedy to reduce a stoppage without investigation the cause.
   2) Immediate action for the M16A1 is:
      a) Tap upward on the bottom of the magazine to insure it is fully seated.
      b) Pull the charging handle fully to the rear (observe for the ejection of a live or expended cartridge) and release it (do not ride the charging handle forward.)
      c) Strike the forward assist assembly to ensure bolt closure.
      d) Attempt to fire the weapon.

6. Q: WHICH MILITARY SERVICE ORIGINALLY ADOPTED THE AR15 AND HAS NOW DESIGNATED THE M16A1 AS ITS STANDARD WEAPON?
A: The U.S. Air Force, in 1962.

7. Q: WHEN WAS THE M16A1 RIFLE ACCEPTED AS THE STANDARD WEAPON FOR THE U.S. ARMY?
A: February 1967.

8. Q: WHAT DO THE FRONT SIGHTS OF OF THE M16A1 ADJUST? ELEVATION OR WINDAGE?
A: Elevation.

9. Q: WHAT DOES THE ACRONYM "BRAS" MEAN?
A: Breath...Relax...Aim...Squeeze.

10. Q: WHAT ARE THE SIX STANDARD SEMI-AUTOMATIC FIRING POSITIONS TAUGHT IN THE RIFLE MARKSMANSHIP PROGRAM FOR THE M16A1 RIFLE?
A: Prone
   Prone supported
   Kneeling
   Kneeling supported
   Standing
   Foxhole

11. Q: WOULD YOU EVER EXCHANGE OR SWITCH BOLTS FROM ONE M16A1 RIFLE TO ANOTHER?
A: No. The head-space is different. The weapon could explode.

12. Q: IF YOUR M16A1 RIFLE HAS WATER IN THE BARREL, WHAT DO YOU DO?
A: Turn muzzle down, pull charging back to unseat chambered round. This will allow the water to flow from the barrel.

13. Q: WHAT POSITION MUST THE SELECTOR LEVER OF THE M16A1 RIFLE BE IN DURING DISASSEMBLY AND ASSEMBLE TO PREVENT DAMAGE TO THE SEAR?
A: Safe.

14. Q: HOW MANY ROUNDS OF AMMUNITION DOES EACH OF THE TWO DIFFERENT MAGAZINES OF THE M16A1 RIFLE HOLD?
A: 20 and 30 rounds.

15. Q: WHAT ARE THE TWO MAIN GROUPS OF THE M16A1 RIFLE?
A: Upper and Lower receiver groups.

16. Q: WHAT IS THE MUZZLE VELOCITY OF THE M16A1 RIFLE?

A: 3,250 feet per second (approximately.)

17. Q: WHAT IS THE MAXIMUM RANGE OF THE M16A1 RIFLE?
A: 2,653 meters.

18. Q: WHAT IS THE MAXIMUM EFFECTIVE RANGE OF THE M16A1 RIFLE?
A: 460 meters.

19. Q: WHAT IS THE WEIGHT OF THE M16A1 RIFLE FULLY LOADED WITH SLING?
A: 7.60 pounds with 20 round magazine.
   7.91 pounds with 30 round magazine.

20. Q: WHAT TYPES OF AMMUNITION DOES THE M16A1 RIFLE USE? Ball (Standard) is one example.
A: Tracer (Standard)
   Blank (Standard)
   Dummy (Standard)

21. Q: WHEN ZEROING YOUR M16A1 RIFLE TO RAISE THE STRIKE OF THE BULLET YOU MUST MOVE THE FRONT SIGHT POST IN WHICH DIRECTION?
A: Downward.

22. Q: WHAT ARE THE THREE POSITIONS OF THE SELECTOR LEVEL OF THE M16A1 RIFLE?
A: Automatic
   Semi-automatic
   Safe

23. Q: WHAT ARE THE FIVE PRINCIPAL POSITIONS FROM WHICH THE RIFLE MAY DELIVER EFFECTIVE AUTOMATIC FIRE WITH THE M16A1 RIFLE?
A: Prone supported.
   Foxhole supported.
   Kneeling supported.
   Standing.
   Underarm positions.

24. Q: PLEASE SHOW ME YOUR WEAPON CARD.
A: Present your weapons card.

25. Q: WHAT DO THE FRONT AND REAR SIGHTS ON THE M16A1 RIFLE ADJUST?
A: Front- elevation.
   Rear- windage.

26. Q: ONCE A SOLDIER'S WEAPON HAS BEEN ZEROED (S)HE CAN HIT HIS POINT OF AIM AT HOW MANY METERS?
A: Two hundred fifty meters.

27. Q: WHAT ARE THE TWO TYPES OF LUBRICATION AUTHORIZED FOR THE M16A1 RIFLE?
A: LSA and (in arctic areas) LAW.

28. Q: IF YOU MUST FIRE THE M16A1 RIFLE ON AUTOMATIC YOU SHOULD, UNDER NORMAL CONDITIONS, FIRE IT IN BURSTS. HOW MANY ROUNDS SHOULD BE EXPENDED WITH EACH BURST?
A: Normally 6-round bursts.

29. Q: WHEN UNLOADING THE M16A1 RIFLE, WHAT IS YOU FIRST ACTION?
A: Place the selector on SAFE.

30. Q: WHEN SHOULD YOUR M16A1 RIFLE BE SECURED AND WHERE?
A: It should be secured when not in use by the individual.
   It should be secured in an approved weapons rack, arms room or other place designated by the commander.

31. Q: IF YOUR WEAPON STOPS FIRING FOR NO OBVIOUS REASON THERE IS AN IMMEDIATE ACTION PROCEDURE YOU SHOULD FOLLOW. THE ACRONYM FOR THIS PROCEDURE IS: S-P-O-R-T-S. EXPLAIN WHAT EACH LETTER OF THE ACRONYM MEANS?
A: S- For SLAP upward on the magazine to make sure it is properly seated.
   P- For PULL the charging handle all the way back.
   O- For OBSERVE ejection of the case or cartridge, eyeball chamber, check for obstruction.
   R- For RELEASE the charging handle if the chamber is clear (don't ride the charging handle forward).
   T- For TAP forward assist.
   S- For SHOOT

32. Q: WHAT IS THE DIFFERENCE BETWEEN THE M16 AND THE M16A1 RIFLE?
A: The M16A1 rifle has a forward assist and a ring at the end of the flash suppressor.

33. Q: WHAT IS THE SUSTAINED RATE OF FIRE FOR THE M16A1 RIFLE?
A: Twelve to fifteen rounds per second.

34. Q: CAN THE GRENADE LAUNCHER BE USED WITH THE M16A1 RIFLE? IF SO, WHAT TYPE?

A: Yes. The M203 Grenade Launcher.

35. Q: WHAT IS MEANT BY "ZEROING" YOUR WEAPON?
A: The number of clicks of elevation and windage you adjust on your rifle to hit the center of a target at a known distance on a day when the wind is not blowing.

36. Q: NAME THE EIGHT STEADY HOLD FACTORS FOR A RIFLE.
A: Grip of the left hand.
    Butt in pocket of shoulder.
    Grip of right hand.
    Right elbow.
    Spot weld.
    Breathing.
    Relaxation.
    Trigger control.

37. Q: WHAT IS A "COOK-OFF"?
A: It is when the barrel of a weapon is so hot from firing that it will automatically chamber the next round or several rounds and fire them.

38. Q: NAME THE THREE POSITIONS OF THE SELECTOR LEVER AND DESCRIBE WHAT THE WEAPON WILL OR WILL NOT DO IN EACH POSITION.
A: Safe- will not fire.
   Semi-automatic- fires one round each time the trigger is pulled.
   Automatic- continues to fire until either the magazine is empty or the trigger is released.

39. Q: WHAT DO YOU LOOK FOR WHEN INSPECTING AMMUNITION?
A: Serious corrosion.
   Dents.
   Dirt.
   Loose bullets.

40. Q: WHAT ARE THE EIGHT STEPS IN THE FIRING CYCLE OF THE M16A1 RIFLE?
A: Feed.
   Chamber.
   Lock.
   Fire.
   Unlock.
   Extract.
   Eject.
   Cock.

41. Q: WHAT IS THE MAIN PURPOSE OF THE FLASH SUPPRESSOR?

A: It breaks up the flash and prevents the weapon from climbing.

42. Q: WHAT BAYONET IS USED WITH THE M16A1 RIFLE?
A: M7

43. Q: WHEN SHOULD YOU CHANGE THE REAR SIGHT OF YOUR M16A1 RIFLE FROM NORMAL TO "L" LONG RANGE?
A: When the target is between 300 and 400 meters away.

44. Q: WHAT IS THE CYCLIC RATE OF FIRE OF THE M16A1 RIFLE?
A: Approximately 700 to 800 rounds per minute.

45. Q: WHAT IS THE MAXIMUM RATE FOR THE M16A1?
A: Semi-automatic- 45 to 65 rounds per minute.
Automatic- 150 to 200 rounds per minute.
Sustained- 12 to 15 rounds per minute.

46. Q: WHAT IS THE FIRST ACTION YOU SHOULD TAKE WHEN CLEANING THE M16A1?
A: Clear the weapon.

47. Q: ON THE FRONT OF THE M16A1 RIFLE, WHAT IS EACH CLICK EQUIVALENT TO IN COMPARISON OF INCHES TO 100 METERS ON THE RANGE?
A: Each click equals 2.8 centimeters (1.1 inches) per every 100 meters of range.

48. Q: WHAT IS MEANT BY THE TERM MAXIMUM EFFECTIVE RANGE?
A: The greatest distance at which a weapon may be expected to fire accurately to inflict casualties or damages.

49. Q: WHAT DOES THE TERM "STOPPAGE" MEAN?
A: Stoppage is the failure of an automatic or semi-automatic firearm to extract or eject a spent case or to load or fire a new round.

50. Q: IF THE WEAPON STILL FAILS TO FIRE, SHOULD YOU REPEAT THE ACTION?
A: No, it must be inspected to determine the cause of the stoppage and appropriate action must be taken.

51. Q: WHEN SHOULD A RIFLE THAT IS SUBJECT TO CAPTURE OR ABANDONMENT, BE DESTROYED?
A: Only by authority of the unit commander.

52. Q: WHAT CLEANING EQUIPMENT SHOULD BE INCLUDED WITH YOU M16A1?
A: Cleaning brush, cleaning rod with swab holder, bore brush, chamber

brush, pipe cleaners, LSA lubricating oil.

53. Q: AT WHAT DISTANCE IS A TARGET SET UP FOR THE PURPOSE OF ZEROING?
A: All preparatory marksmanship is conducted on the 25 meter range.

54. Q: HOW DOES TRAJECTORY AFFECT SIGHT ALIGNMENT?
A: It will appear to have a curved trajectory.

55. Q: WHAT FIELD MANUAL DO YOU REFER TO FOR THE M16A1?
A: FM 23-9.

56. Q: WHAT IS THE BLANK FIRING ATTACHMENT?
A: The M15E1.

57. Q: WHAT TRAINING MANUAL DO YOU REFER TO FOR CLEANING YOUR M16A1?
A: The TM 9-1005-249-10 and TM 9-1005-249-34.

Military Customs & Courtesies

1. Q: WHAT SHOULD YOU DO WHEN THE NATIONAL ANTHEM OF A FOREIGN COUNTRY IS PLAYED?
A: Come to the position of attention and salute.

2. Q: WHEN APPROACHING AN OFFICER, AT WHAT POINT SHOULD YOU SALUTE?
A: At six to thirty paces or when eye-to-eye contact has been made.

3. Q: ON THE FOURTH OF JULY, WHAT TAKES PLACE AT 1200 HOURS ON MOST MILITARY POSTS?
A: A 50 gun salute is fired. It is referred to as "Salute to the Union."

4. Q: WHEN IS IT ALLOWED TO WEAR A HAT INSIDE A BUILDING?
A: When under arms.

5. Q: YOU HAVE A PLATOON IN FORMATION AND AT EASE. AN OFFICER APPROACHES TO SPEAK TO YOU. WHAT IS YOUR ACTION?
A: Call the platoon to attention and salute.

6. Q: YOU ARE IN CHARGE OF DETAIL AND ARE IN A VEHICLE AND ARE PASSING THE COLORS AT RETREAT. WHAT ARE YOUR ACTIONS AND/OR YOUR DETAIL'S ACTIONS?
A: Tell the driver to halt, dismount and render hand salute while detail remains sitting at attention.

7. Q: WHAT IS THE PROPER WAY TO WALK WITH AN OFFICER?
A: Walk on the left, 1/2 pace to the rear.

8. Q: WHAT ARMY REGULATION GOVERNS THE NUMBER OF GUN SALUTES AN INDIVIDUAL IS TO BE AFFORDED?
A: AR 600-25.

9. Q: STATE TWO INSTANCES IN WHICH SOLDIERS WHO ARE "UNDER ARMS" UNCOVER.
A: Seated as a member of, or in attendance on, a court or board.
Entering a place of divine worship.
Indoors when not on duty.
In attendance at an official reception.

10. Q: WHEN PEOPLE OF DIFFERENT RANKS ARE IN A MILITARY VEHICLE AND THE VEHICLE STOPS TO ALLOW ALL INDIVIDUALS TO EXIT- WHO GETS OUT FIRST?
A: The senior officer (enlisted) gets out first.

11. Q: DESCRIBE THE PROCEDURES FOR REPORTING TO AN OFFICER IN HIS OFFICE.
A: Approach within two steps of the desk.
Halt, salute and report- hold salute until it is returned.
State your business.
When business is completed:
Salute- Hold salute until it is returned.
Make an about face and depart in a military manner.

12. Q: WHEN ARE YOU REQUIRED TO SALUTE A FOREIGN OFFICER?
A: When both of you are in uniform.

13. Q: WHAT HONORS ARE FOREIGN MILITARY PERSONS RENDERED?
A: Honors due to their actual rank or its United States equivalent.

14. Q: MAY AN OFFICER DETAILED TO DUTY AS AN INSPECTOR GENERAL ASSUME COMMAND WHILE SO DETAILED?
A: No.

15. Q: WHEN IS THE UNIFORM HAT OR CAP RAISED AS A FORM OF SALUTE?
A: The hat or cap will never be raised in the form of a salute.

16. Q: HOW WILL OFFICERS OF THE SAME GRADE SHOW RESPECT?
A: By a salute.

17. Q: WHAT TYPE OF GUN SALUTE IS AFFORDED THE PRESIDENT, EX-PRESIDENT, OR PRESIDENT-ELECT ON ARRIVAL OR DEPARTURE?
A: A 21-gun salute.

18. Q: WHEN DO MILITARY PERSONNEL SALUTE UNCASED COLORS?
A: When colors are six steps from them and they hold the salute until the colors are six steps beyond them.

19. Q: ARE VEHICLES REQUIRED TO HALT WHEN THE NATIONAL ANTHEM IS PLAYED?
A: Yes. Personnel riding in passenger cars will halt, dismount and salute or render appropriate honors. Personnel riding in a bus or in a truck will remain in the vehicle while the senior person dismounts and salutes.

20. Q: YOU ARE INDOORS AND THE NATIONAL ANTHEM IS PLAYED. WHAT DO YOU DO?
A: Stand at attention, face music, do not salute unless under arms.

21. Q: WHAT MAY A SOLDIER NOT DO DURING POLITICAL ELECTIONS?
A: Use his official authority or influence for the purpose of interfering with an election or affecting the course of its outcome.
   Be a candidate and hold civil office.
   A member on active duty cannot actively participate in partisan political management, campaigns or conventions.

23. Q: WHAT IS MEANT BY MILITARY DISCIPLINE?
A: It is a state of individual and group training that creates a mental attitude resulting in correct conduct and automatic obedience to military law under all conditions.

24. Q: HOW CAN SOMEONE ON ACTIVE DUTY PARTICIPATE IN AN ELECTION?
A: Register, vote, and express his personal opinion on political issues and candidates: but not as a representative of the Armed Forces. Attend partisan as well as nonpartisan meetings or rallies as a spectator when not in uniform.

25. Q: WHAT IS THE "SALUTE TO THE UNION?"
A: The "Salute to the Union" is a 50-gun salute celebrating the Declaration of Independence. One gun is fired for each State at noon on 4 July at military posts.

26. Q: HOW WOULD A FEMALE WARRANT OFFICER BE ADDRESSED?
A: She would be addressed as either "Miss" or "Mrs."

27. Q: IS THERE ANY EXCEPTION TO THE "JUNIOR ON THE LEFT" COURTESY? IF SO, WHAT IS IT?
A: Yes. During inspection of troops.

28. Q: HOW DO YOU SALUTE WITH AN ORGANIZATIONAL COLOR OR STANDARD?
A: You dip it in the form of a salute.

29. Q: ARE DESIGNATED REPRESENTATIVES OF OFFICIALS ENTITLED TO HONORS AFFORDED THE SAME HONORS AS THE REPRESENTED OFFICIAL?
A: No. the representative will be afforded honors according to his/her rank.

30. Q: WHAT DO WE MEAN BY MILITARY COURTESY?
A: It is the respect and consideration shown by the members of the military to each other.

31. Q: WHAT ACTION IS TAKEN WHEN THE FLAG IS LOWERED?
A: Military personnel salute and civilian personnel place hand over the heart.

32. Q: WHAT IS MEANT BY "UNDER ARMS?"
A: It is carrying the Arms or having them attached to your person by a sling or holster.

33. Q: IF YOUR CHAPLAIN WAS A LTC HOW WOULD YOU ADDRESS HIM?
A: Chaplain (regardless of rank.)

34. Q: WHEN SPEAKING WITH A FEMALE OFFICER, WHAT TERM OF ADDRESS IS USED?
A: Ma'am.

35. Q: WHAT IS MEANT BY "CHAIN OF COMMAND?"
A: It is the succession of Commanders, superior to subordinate, through which command is exercised.

36. Q: THE VICE PRESIDENT, SECRETARY OF DEFENSE, SECRETARY OF THE ARMY AND SEVERAL OTHER DISTINGUISHED INDIVIDUALS ARE AUTHORIZED A CERTAIN NUMBER OF GUN SALUTES WHEN THEY AR-

RIVE AND DEPART. HOW MANY GUN SALUTES ARE REQUIRED FOR THE INDIVIDUALS LISTED ABOVE?
A: A 19 gun salute.

37. Q: WHAT IS THE DEFINITION OF MILITARY RANK?
A: The relative position of degree of precedence on military persons which marks their station and confers eligibility to exercise command or authority in the military service within the limits prescribed by law.

38. Q: IF YOU ARE IN A ROOM AND AN OFFICER ENTERS THE ROOM, WHAT WOULD YOU DO?
A: Call attention and report if others are in the room. If alone, come to attention and report.

39. Q: WHAT IS CONSIDERED THE MOST IMPORTANT OF ALL MILITARY COURTESIES?
A: The salute.

40. Q: WHEN DO YOU SALUTE?
A: 1) When the NATIONAL ANTHEM, TO THE COLORS, RUFFLES AND FLOURISHES, OR HAIL TO THE CHIEF is played.
  2) When the national colors or standard passes by.
  3) On ceremonial occasions.
  4) In all official greetings to warrant & commissioned officers.
  5) At Reveille.
  6) When in sight of the flag or sound of the music.
  7) During the rendering of honors.
  8) When passing by uncased colors when outdoors.
  9) When in doubt as to whether or not to salute.

41. Q: WHAT SHOULD YOU DO WHEN THE NATIONAL ANTHEM OF A FOREIGN COUNTRY IS PLAYED?
A: Come to the position of attention and salute.

42. Q: WHAT POSITION IS ASSUMED WHEN "RETREAT" IS PLAYED?
A: The position of "attention" is assumed when not in formation. The position of parade rest when in a military formation.

43. Q: WHEN DO YOU NOT SALUTE AN OFFICER?
A: When on a work detail.
   When outdoors, except when reporting to a senior, or when on guard.
   When in formation, unless commanded to do so.

44. Q: DO YOU SALUTE WHEN IN A VEHICLE?
A: Yes. Except drivers of military or civilian vehicles are not required to salute at times when a safety hazard will be created. All personnel should be alert to distinguish and salute vehicles bearing the Secretary of the Army, Secretary of

Defense, General officers, or Admiral's automobile plates.

45. Q: IS AN OFFICER REQUIRED TO RETURN THE SALUTE OF AN ENLISTED MAN WHO SALUTES OUTSIDE AND GIVES THE GREETING OF THE DAY?
A: Yes.

46. Q: ON WHAT OCCASION, WHEN REPORTING, IS AN OFFICER NOT REQUIRED TO RETURN YOUR SALUTE?
A: At pay call.

47. Q: WHO ENTERS A VEHICLE FIRST?
A: Junior first, others in inverse order of rank.

48. Q: ON MEMORIAL DAY, WHAT TAKES PLACE AT 1200 HRS ON MOST POSTS?
A: A 21 gun salute is fired.

49. Q: IF YOU WERE IN A MESS HALL AND AN OFFICER WALKED IN AND YOU NOTICED HIM FIRST, WHAT COMMAND WOULD YOU GIVE?
A: At ease.

50. Q: YOU ARE IN CHARGE OF A DETAIL. RIDING IN THE FRONT SEAT OF A 2 1/2 TON. YOUR DETAIL IS IN THE BACK. A GENERAL OFFICER APPROACHES. WHO SALUTES?
A: NCO or person in charge of the detail.

51. Q: WHAT, IF ANY, IS THE MINIMUM PAY GRADE YOU MUST BE TO HOLD ELECTED CIVIL OFFICE?
A: No one on active duty can hold elected civil office.

52. Q: WHEN ARE YOU REQUIRED TO SALUTE FOREIGN OFFICERS?
A: When both of you are in uniform.

53. Q: WHAT REGULATION COVERS ARMY COMMAND POLICY AND POLICY PROCEDURES?
A: AR 600-20.

54. Q: WHO COMMANDS A MEDICAL UNIT?
A: The senior Medical Corp officer assigned or attached to a medical unit which is temporarily deployed to receive and treat patients, will assume command.

55. Q: WHO IS INELIGIBLE FOR COMMAND OF POST OR ACTIVITY?
A: 1) Any person under arrest.
    2) Quartered there, but has headquarter or office elsewhere.
    3) Not permanently assigned.

56. Q: WHAT IS AN ARMY SPECIALIST?
A: A specialist is a selected person appointed to discharge duties requiring a high degree of special skill.

57. Q: MAY A CIVILIAN EXERCISE COMMAND?
A: A civilian may not exercise command. However, a civilian may be designated to exercise general supervision over an Army installation or activity under the command of a military supervisor.

58. Q: WHEN IS THE PLEDGE OF ALLEGIANCE RECITED IN MILITARY FORMATIONS OR IN MILITARY CEREMONIES?
A: Never.

59. Q: WHAT MUST FOLLOW THE PLAYING OF A FOREIGN NATIONAL ANTHEM?
A: The National Anthem of the United States.

60. Q: WHAT IS THE TIME INTERVAL BETWEEN SOUNDS OF A CANNON SALUTE AT AT FUNERAL?
A: 5 seconds.

61. Q: IS A SALUTE REQUIRED WHEN AN ENLISTED MAN IS IN MILITARY ATTIRE BUT THE OFFICER IS IN CIVILIAN ATTIRE?
A: No.

62. Q: ARE SALUTES REQUIRED IN PUBLIC PLACES SUCH AS THEATERS AND OUTDOOR SPORTING EVENTS?
A: No.

63. Q: WHEN OFFICERS ARE ENTERING A BOAT, WHO ENTERS FIRST?
A: The lowest ranking officer.

64. Q: WHAT POSITION IS ASSUMED WHEN "RETREAT" IS PLAYED?
A: The position of "attention" is assumed when not in formation. The position of parade rest when in a military formation.

65. Q: HOW MANY GUN SALUTES IS THE...................... ENTITLED?

A. **Grade or Titles**	**Number of Gun Salutes**
President	21
Ex-President or President-Elect	21
Vice President	19
Speaker of the House of Representatives	19
Premier or Prime Minister	19
Secretary of Defense	19
Cabinet members, Governor of a state, Chief	

Justice of the United States	19
Secretary of the Army	19
Chairman, Joint Chief of Staff	19
Chief of Staff, United States Army	19
General of the Army	19
Generals	17
Lieutenant Generals	15
Major Generals	13
Brigadier Generals	11

The above is a list of persons who are entitled to honors, together with number of guns. AR 600-25

Origin of the Hand Salute

Many Army customs originated long ago. The hand salute, for example, is so old that its origin is uncertain. Some students of history say it began in late Roman times, when assassinations were common. People who wanted to see public officials had to come before them with their right hands raised to show that they did not hold weapons. In medieval times, knights in armor always raised their visors with the right hand when meeting a comrade. This practice gradually became a way of showing respect, and in early American history sometimes involved removing the hat. This was later modified to touching the hat, and still later became the hand salute used today.

Position of Honor

As part of military courtesy, soldiers always walk or sit to the left of seniors. This is another custom with a long past. Soldiers fought for centuries with swords, and, because most men were right-handed, the heaviest fighting occurred on the right. The shield was carried on the left arm, and the left side became defensive. Soldiers were proud of their fighting honor. When an officer or senior enlisted soldier walked on the right, he is symbolically filling post of honor. You should walk on the senior's left, and stop when he does.

Military Courtesy

Courteous behavior is essential in human relations, whether civilian or military. The distinction between civilian courtesy and military courtesy is that military courtesies were developed in a military atmosphere and have become customs and traditions of the service. Most forms of military courtesy have some counterpart in civilian life. For example, you are required to say "sir" when you talk to an officer. Throughout our history, young men and women were taught to say "sir" when speaking to an older man. The use of the word "sir" is also common in the business world, in the address of letters, and in any well-ordered institution. Military courtesy is not a one-way street. Enlisted personnel must be courteous to officers, and officers are expected to return the courtesy. Officers respect soldiers as individuals, just as we respect officers as individuals. Without this basis of mutual respect, there can be no military courtesy, and disharmony will result. In the final analysis, military courtesy is the respect shown to each other by members of the same profession, and is also a form of respect for the nation. Enlisted personnel show military courtesy to their officers because they respect the position of responsibility held by the officer. Officers, on the other hand, respect their personnel because they know the responsibility the personnel have in carrying out orders. Military courtesy also includes salutes, the correct use of titles, respect for the flag and the national anthem, and military funerals.

Other Courtesies to Individuals

1) military personnel are customarily addressed in official correspondence by their full titles. In conversation and unofficial correspondence, Army personnel are addressed as follows:
    All general officers— "General."
    Colonels and lieutenant colonels— "Colonel."
    Majors— "Major."
    Captains— "Captain."
    All lieutenants— "Lieutenant."
    All chaplains— "Chaplain."
    Cadets— "Mister."
    Officer candidates— "Candidate."
    Warrant officers— "Mister," "Mrs.," or "Miss."
    Sergeants major— "Sergeant Major"
    All other sergeants— "Sergeant."
    All specialists— "Specialist."
    Privates and privates first class— "Private."

b) The term of respect, "sir," is used when speaking to officers and civilian officials. Each sentence or statement should be either preceded or terminated with the word, "sir," but should not be used both before and after the statement. When speaking with a female officer, the term "ma'am" instead of "sir" is used. When answering a telephone on a military installation, always assume that the caller is an officer and respond accordingly. Some units have mottoes that they prescribe for answering the telephone, but the normal procedure is to identify the unit and yourself, and end with "sir." Giving the company and battalion is usually sufficient to identify the unit.

c) Conversation carried on in the presence of troops should be formal and proper, and proper titles should be used. When not in the presence of troops, seniors may address juniors by their first or last name, but this does not give the junior the privilege of addressing the senior in any way other than by his proper title. Individuals of the same grade generally address one another by name.

Uncovering

    a) Officers and enlisted personnel under arms uncover only when:
        1) In attendance at a court or board. (Prisoner guards do not uncover.)
        2) Entering places of divine worship.
        3) Indoors, when not at a place of duty.
        4) In attendance at an official reception.
    b) When armed, the cap is removed indoors. When out of doors, the cap is never removed or raised as a form of salutation.

Actions When an Officer Enters a Facility or Vehicle

    a) When an officer enters a room, stand at attention until the officer either directs otherwise or leaves. When more than one person is present, the first to see the officer commands, "Attention". When a noncommissioned officer enters a barracks, if he has information or instruction for personnel living in the barracks, he will call, "At ease," loud enough for all those present to hear.

    b) When an officer enters an office, workshop or place of recreation, personnel engaged in an activity do not come to attention unless the officer speaks to them. A junior comes to attention when addressed by a senior, except in the transaction of routine business between individuals at work.

    c) When an officer enters a mess, the mess will be called to "at ease" by the first person who sees the officer unless that officer directs otherwise, or unless a more senior officer is already present in the mess. The person in charge reports to the officer. The personnel remain seated at ease and continue eating unless the officer directs otherwise. An individual directly addressed should rise to attention unless seated on a bench instead of a chair, in which case he stops eating and sits at attention until the conversation is ended.

    d) When an officer or noncommissioned officer enters a crowed hallway or similar area where troops are taking a break or standing in a waiting line, the first person to see the officer or noncommissioned officer should call, "At ease" and "Make way," so those present will move to the sides of the hallway and allow passage.

    e) When accompanying a senior, the junior walks or rides on his left.

    f) Upon entering a vehicle, the junior enters first and others follow in inverse order of rank. Upon leaving a vehicle, the senior leaves first and other follow in order of rank.

    g) When a commanding officer enters an office for the first time each day, "Attention" will be called by the first person noticing the officer. If a higher commander enters, "Attention" is called again.

Meaning of the Hand Salute

    a) The salute is a greeting between military personnel. It is a military way of saying, "Hello, how are you?" In fact, it is customary to say, "Good morning, Sir," Good afternoon, Sir," or "Good evening, Sir," when you salute an officer. Usually it is proper for officers of the same rank to salute each other when they meet, because it is the military way of saying "Hello." Sometimes, of course, you will use the hand salute to honor the colors. Then the salute is used as a mark of respect for you country.

    b) The way we salute is important because it tells a lot about us as soldiers. If we salute proudly and smartly, it shows that we have pride in ourselves and pride in our unit and country. It shows that we have confidence in our abilities as soldiers. A sloppy salute, on the other hand, shows that we lack confidence, or that we don't understand the meaning of the salute, or that we are ashamed of our unit and ourselves.

    c) When reporting or rendering courtesy to an individual, turn the head and eyes toward the person addressed and simultaneously salute. In this situation, the actions are executed without command. The salute is initiated by the subordinate at the appropriate time and terminated when returned.

    d) The hand salute may be executed while marching. When double-timing, individuals must come to quick time before saluting.

NOTE: When marching a formation at double time, only the individual in charge assumes quick time and salutes.

    e) It is improper to salute with any object in the right hand or with a cigarette, cigar, or pipe in the mouth.

Whom to Salute

Salute all commissioned officers and warrant officers of the Armed Forces and of allied nations when you recognize them as such. Do not salute noncommissioned officers.

When to Salute

All Army personnel in uniform are required to salute at all times when they meet and recognize persons entitled to the salute, except when a salute would be inappropriate or impractical (e.g., in public conveyance such as trains or buses, in public places such as theaters, or when driving a vehicle.) The rendering of the salute is also required:

    1) When the national anthem, "To the Colors," or "Hail to the Chief" is played outdoors. (When played indoors, all present stand at attention.)
    2) When the national colors pass by.
    3) At reveille, when within sight of the flag or hearing of the music.
    4) During the rendering or honors (during cannon salutes.)
    5) When passing by uncased colors outdoors.
    6) When pledging allegiance to the flag.

    b) When an officer approaches, a salute is rendered only once if the officer remains in the immediate vicinity and no conversation takes place. If a conversation takes place, the soldier again salutes the officer on departing or when the officer leaves.

c) Exception to the general rule prescribing the salute are indicated in specific rules given in subsequent paragraphs. In general, one <u>does not</u> salute when:

    1) At work.

    2) Indoors, except when reporting to an officer or when on duty as a guard. (The term "outdoors" includes such buildings as drill halls, gymnasiums, and other structures used for drill or exercise of troops. Theater marquees, covered walks, and other shelters open on the sides to the weather and where a hat may be worn are also considered outdoors. The term "indoors" includes offices, hallways, kitchens, orderly rooms, recreation rooms, washrooms, and squad rooms.)

    3) A prisoner.

    4) The rendition of the salute is obviously inappropriate. (Example: A person carrying articles with both hands, or otherwise so occupied as to make saluting impractical, is not required to salute a senior or to return the salute of a junior.) any case not covered by specific instructions, or in case of reasonable doubt, the salute will be rendered.

Salute in Vehicles

Salutes are not required to be rendered by or to personnel in vehicles. An exception is made for gate guards, who will salute recognized officers in official vehicles only (AR 600-25). All personnel will salute general officers in official vehicles.

Saluting in Groups

a) <u>Information.</u> Individuals in formation do not salute or return salutes except at the commands, "Present arms," or "Hand, salute." The individual in charge salutes and acknowledges salutes for the entire formation. Commanders of organizations or detachments which are not a part of a larger formation salute officers of higher grades by bringing the organization or detachment to attention before saluting. An individual in formation at ease or at rest comes to attention when addressed by an officer.

b) <u>Not in Formation.</u> Upon the approach of an officer, a group of individuals not in formation is called to attention by the first person noticing the officer, and all come smartly to attention and salute. Members of details at work and individuals participating in games do not salute. The individual in charge of a work detail, if not actively engaged, salutes or acknowledges salutes for the entire detail. A unit resting alongside a road does not come to attention upon the approach of an officer; however, if the officer addresses an individual or group, the individual or group comes to attention and remains at attention (unless otherwise ordered) until the termination of the conversation, at which time they salute the officer.

The Army Song

a) The U.S. Army is the only service with an official marching song. It was adapted from the music of "The Caisson Song," written about 1908. The official Army Song was formally dedicated by the Secretary of the Army on Veterans Day, 11 November 1956.

b) In addition to standing while the national anthem is being played, audiences render honors while state songs, school songs, and other symbolic songs are being played. Accordingly, Army personnel will stand at attention whenever the official Army song is played.

Retreat

a) The bugle call sounded at retreat was first used in the French army and dates back to the Crusades. When you hear it, you are listening to a beautiful melody that has come to symbolize the finest qualities of the soldiers of nearly 900 years. Retreat has always been played at sunset, and its original purpose was to notify the sentries to start challenging until sunrise, and to tell the rank and file to go to their quarters and stay there. In our times the ceremony remains as a tradition. When outdoors and retreat is played, face toward the flag and stand at <u>attention</u>. If the flag is not within sight, face toward the music.

b) Retreat is followed by the playing of "To the Colors." On the first note of "To the Colors," execute the hand salute,, present arms, or hand salute at sling arms, whichever is appropriate.

Salute to the Colors

Military personnel passing an uncased national color salutes at six steps distance and hold the salute until it has passed six steps beyond them. Small flags carried by individuals, such as those carried by civilian spectators at a parade, are not saluted.

General Orders

a) I will guard everything within the limits of my post and quit my post only when properly relieved.

b) I will obey my special orders and perform all my duties in a military manner.

c) I will report violations of my special orders, emergencies, and anything not covered in my instructions to the commander of the relief.

Awards

1. Q: WHAT IS THE HIGHEST AWARD GIVEN BY THE ARMY IN TIME OF WAR?

A: The Medal of Honor.

2. Q: TO WHOM IS THE PURPLE HEART AWARDED?
A: To military or civilian personnel wounded in action against an armed enemy.

3. Q: WHO MUST AWARD THE MEDAL OF HONOR?
A: The President of the United States, approved by Congress.

4. Q: WHAT IS THE SECOND HIGHEST AWARD IN THE ARMED FORCES?
A: The Distinguished Service Cross.

5. Q: FOR WHAT IS A "CLASP" USED?
A: To indicate a second or subsequent award.

6. Q: WHAT ARE THE FIVE HIGHEST AWARDS WITHIN THE U.S. ARMY?
A: Medal of Honor
Distinguished Service Cross
Distinguished Service Medal
Silver Star
Legion of Merit

7. Q: MOST OF THE PRESENT DAY DECORATIONS DATE BACK TO THE TWO WORLD WARS. WHICH MEDAL DATES BACK TO THE REVOLUTIONARY WAR AND IS STILL AWARDED AND WORN TODAY. ALSO, WHO WAS THE FIRST MAN TO PRESENT THE AWARD.
A: George Washington was the first man to award The Purple Heart.

8. Q: WHO CAN PREPARE RECOMMENDATIONS FOR AWARDS?
A: Any individual having knowledge of an outstanding act or achievement.

9. Q: WHAT IS MEANT BY "ABOVE AND BEYOND THE CALL OF DUTY?"
A: It is the acceptance of existing danger or extraordinary responsibility with praiseworthy fortitude and exemplary courage which is not as a rule expected of a person.

10. Q: THE GOLD BAR WORN FOUR INCHES FROM THE BOTTOM OF THE RIGHT SLEEVE ON A DRESS UNIFORM DENOTES WHAT?
A: This bar denotes six months service in a wartime overseas Theater.

11. Q: WHICH ARMY REGULATIONS TELLS YOU EXACTLY WHAT CIVILIAN DECORATIONS AND RIBBONS MAY BE WORN WITH THE UNIFORMS?
A: AR 672-5-1.

12. Q: WHICH AWARD IS GIVEN FOR BEHAVIOR, EFFICIENCY, AND FIDELITY DURING ENLISTED STATUS ON ACTIVE FEDERAL MILITARY SERVICE FOR THREE YEARS OF SERVICE?
A: The Good Conduct Medal.

13. Q: FOR WHAT IS THE SOLDIERS MEDAL AWARDED?
A: For distinguished act of heroism not involving actual contact with an armed enemy.

14. Q: FOR WHAT IS THE ARMY COMMENDATION MEDAL GIVEN?
A: For meritorious service and acts of heroism when acts of courage do not meet requirements for the Soldiers Medal. Also for circumstances of a lesser degree than required for the Bronze Star Medal.

15. Q: TO WHOM IS THE ARMY SERVICE RIBBON AWARDED?
A: Any member of the U.S. Army who has successfully complete initial entry training.

16. Q: WHAT ARMY REGULATION DEALS WITH MILITARY AWARDS?
A: AR 672-5-1.

17. Q: IN WHAT YEAR WAS THE SOLDIER'S MEDAL ESTABLISHED?
A: Act of Congress, 2 July 1926.

18. Q: WHO HAS THE AUTHORITY TO AWARD THE GOOD CONDUCT MEDAL?
A: Unit Commanders are authorized to award Good Conduct Medals to enlisted personnel serving their commands.

19. Q: TRUE OR FALSE? AN INDIVIDUAL IS AUTOMATICALLY ENTITLED

TO AN AWARD UPON DEPARTURE FORM AN ASSIGNMENT?
A: False.

20. Q: TO WHOM MAY THE SOLDIER'S MEDAL BE AWARDED TO?
A: It may be awarded to any person of the Armed Forces of the United States?

21. Q: THERE ARE SEVEN CATEGORIES OF INDIVIDUALS AWARDS, NAME FOUR.
A: a) Decorations
   b) Good Conduct Medal
   c) Badges
   d) Service Medals
   e) Certificates
   f) Letters
   g) Tabs

22. Q: WHAT IS THE LEGION OF MERIT AWARDED FOR?
A: For any member of the Armed Forces who has distinguished himself by exceptionally meritorious conduct in the performance of outstanding services.

23. Q: RECOMMENDATIONS FOR DECORATIONS SHOULD BE SUBMITTED ON DA FORM 2496 OR DA FORM 638?
A: DA FORM 638.

24. Q: WHAT IS THE DRIVER AND MECHANIC BADGE AWARDED FOR?
A: It is awarded for the high degree of skill in the operation and maintenance of motor vehicles.

25. Q: TRUE OR FALSE? MERITORIOUS SERVICE MEDAL IS AWARDED TO ANY MEMBER OF THE ARMED FORCES OF THE UNITED STATES WHO IS IN A NONCOMBAT AREA AFTER 16 JANUARY 1969?
A: True.

26. Q: WHAT ARE THE COLORS OF THE GOOD CONDUCT MEDAL?
A: Red and white.

27. Q: WHAT IS THE PURPOSE OF AN AWARD?
A: To recognize heroism, meritorious achievement or meritorious service.

28. Q: WHAT IS THE MEANING OF MEDAL?
A: A term is used in either of two ways; to include the three categories of awards namely: decorations, Good Conduct Medals; or refer to the distinctive physical device of metal and ribbon which constitutes the tangible evidence of an award.

29. Q: WHAT IS A SERVICE STAR?
A: The Service Star is a bronze or silver five-pointed star 2/16 of an inch in

diameter.

30. Q: WHAT IS THE PURPOSE OF THE DEPARTMENT OF DEFENSE MERITORIOUS AWARD?
A: To award outstanding organizations which have contributed in an outstanding manner to the National Defense effort.

31. Q: WHO MAY BE AWARDED THE HUMANITARIAN SERVICE MEDAL?
A: Awarded to service members who directly participate in a DOD approved Military Act or operation of a humanitarian nature.

32. Q: WHAT IS THE COMMENDATION STAR?
A: The Commendation Star is a bronze five point star 3/16 of an inch in diameter.

33. Q: DO NUMERALS USED IN CONJUNCTION WITH THE NPDR (NCO PROFESSIONAL DEVELOPMENT RIBBON) DENOTE SECOND AND SUCCEEDING AWARDS?
A: Yes. Once a service member has been awarded the basic service ribbon, a #2 will signify BNOC with the appropriate numerals awarded to denote completion of higher level NCO development courses.

34. Q: DO NUMERALS USED IN CONJUNCTION WITH OVERSEAS SERVICE RIBBON (OSR) DENOTE SECOND AND SUCCEEDING AWARDS?
A: Yes, numerals will be used to denote second and subsequent awards of the OSR.

35. Q: IF AN INDIVIDUAL HAS A SERVICE MEDAL, WHICH RECOGNIZES HIS OVERSEAS TOUR, CAN HE WEAR THE OVERSEAS SERVICE RIBBON FOR THE SAME OVERSEAS TOUR?
A: No, the overseas service ribbon will not be awarded for overseas service recognized with another service medal.

36. Q: NAME THE THREE RIBBONS THAT BECAME EFFECTIVE 1 AUGUST 1981.
A: Overseas Service Ribbon
Army Service Ribbon
NCO Professional Development Ribbon

37. Q: WHO HAS THE AUTHORITY TO AUTHORIZE AN INDIVIDUAL TO WEAR AND ACCEPT FOREIGN DECORATIONS?
A: a) Headquarters, Department of the Army.
b) Commanders of major overseas command reporting directly to HQ DA.

38. Q: WHEN CAN A COMMANDER ISSUE A CERTIFICATE OF ACHIEVEMENT?
A: When an individual's faithful service, acts, or achievements deserve recogni-

tion; but fail the standards required for decorations.

39. Q: WHEN DOES AN INDIVIDUAL RECEIVE A GOOD CONDUCT MEDAL CERTIFICATE?
A: a) Concurrent with the first award of the GCMDL earned on or after 1 Jan 81.
   b) Concurrent with retirement on or after 1 Jan 81.

40. Q: CAN AN OFFICER WEAR THE ARMY SERVICE RIBBON?
A: Yes, upon successful completion of his/her resident basic/orientation course.

41. Q: THERE ARE FOUR LEVELS OF NCO PROFESSIONAL DEVELOPMENT, NAME EACH LEVEL AND THE COURSES OF EACH LEVEL?
   a) Primary Level- Primary NCO Courses, Combat Arms (PNCOC), Primary Leadership Courses (PLC) and Primary Technical Courses (Service School (PTC)).
   b) Basic Level- Basic NCO Course, Combat Arms (BNCOC) and basic Technical Courses (Service School-BTC)
   c) Advanced Level- Advanced NCO Course (Service School- ANCOC).
   d) Senior Level- First Sergeants Course and Sergeant Major Academy.

42. Q: WHO IS ELIGIBLE FOR AWARD OF THE NCO PROFESSIONAL DEVELOPMENT RIBBON, ARMY SERVICE RIBBON, AND OVERSEAS SERVICE RIBBON?
A: Any member of the active Army, Army National Guard, and Army Reserve on 1 Aug 1981, who is otherwise qualified.

43. Q: IF A FULLY QUALIFIED PERSON IS SCHEDULED FOR SEPARATION FROM ACTIVE FEDERAL MILITARY SERVICE, HOW FAR IN ADVANCE CAN HE/SHE RECEIVE THE GOOD CONDUCT AWARD?
A: The award can be given up to 30 days prior to the soldier's departure in route to a separation processing installation in CONUS or overseas.

44. Q: IF AN INDIVIDUAL HAS RECEIVED ANY ARTICLE 15'S, DOES THIS AUTOMATICALLY DISQUALIFY HIM FROM RECEIVING A GOOD CONDUCT AWARD?
A: No, while any record of non-judicial punishment could be in conflict with recognizing the soldier's service as exemplary, such record would not be viewed as automatically disqualifying.

45. Q: NAME THE FOUR TYPES OF BADGES.
A: Combat and special skill badges.
   Marksmanship badges
   Identification badges
   Locally authorized badges

46. Q: IS THERE A TIME LIMIT FOR RECOMMENDING SOMEONE FOR A MILITARY DECORATION?
A: Yes, a recommendation for an award of a military decoration must be entered administratively into military channels within two years.

47. Q: WHAT IS THE OBJECTIVE OF THE DEPARTMENT OF ARMY MILITARY AWARDS PROGRAMS??
A: The objective is to provide tangible recognition for acts of valor, exceptional service or achievement, special skills or qualifications, and acts of heroism not involving actual combat.

48. Q: WHO CAN AWARD AN INDIVIDUAL A DECORATION AFTER THEIR RECOMMENDATION HAS BEEN LOST?
A: The Secretary of the Army.

Duty Rosters

1. Q: TO WHAT DOES A NUMBER IN PARENTHESIS IMMEDIATELY FOLLOWING A PERSON'S NAME REFER?
A: An explanatory remark on the reverse of the roster.

2. Q: WHAT ARMY REGULATION GOVERNS DUTY ROSTERS?
A: AR 220-45.

3. Q: HOW ARE SOLDIERS CHOSEN TO PERFORM A DETAIL?
A: The person longest of the duty roster (highest number), will be the next person detailed. When such person is not available, the person on the roster who is next longest off the duty roster will be detailed.

4. Q: DIAGONAL LINES IN THE RIGHT CORNER OF ANY BLOCK INDICATE WHAT?
A: Performance of the duty on that date.

5. Q: WHAT IS THE PURPOSE OF A DUTY ROSTER?
A: To record the duty performed by each person in an organization in order to make an equitable determination of duty assignments.

6. Q: HOW ARE WEEKEND/HOLIDAY PERIODS INDICATED ON A CONSOLIDATED ROSTER?
A: By a system of vertical red lines or by indicating the dates, numbers and diagonal lines in red.

7. Q: WHICH DATE WILL ALWAYS BE ENTERED IN THE "TO (DATE)" SECTION ON A DA FORM 6?
A: The date of the last detail covered by that roster and will be entered only when the roster is closed.

8. Q: WHICH DA FORM IS USED FOR THE DUTY ROSTER?
A: DA FORM 6.

9. Q: WHAT LETTER WILL INDICATE THAT THOSE ELIGIBLE FOR DETAIL COULD NOT BE SELECTED BECAUSE OF PREVIOUS DETAIL OR OTHER DUTY?
A: "D" (Indicating "duty").

10. Q: WHAT ARE THE THREE ABBREVIATIONS AUTHORIZED ON A DUTY ROSTER?
A: "A" -Authorized absence.
"D" -Duty.
"U" -Unauthorized absence.

11. Q: WHICH ARMY REGULATIONS GOVERN DISPOSAL OF DUTY ROSTER FILES?
A: AR 340-2
AR 340-6
AR 340-18-1

12. Q: PFC ROBERTS WAS ASSIGNED TO YOUR UNIT ON THE 12TH OF MAY. WHAT DAY WOULD HE BE ELIGIBLE FOR DUTY?
A: The 13th of May.

13. Q: A UNIT YOU HAVE JUST BEEN ASSIGNED TO IS A SHIFT WORKING UNIT. MAY THE COMMANDER ESTABLISH PROCEDURES TO SELECT DUTIES, OTHER THAN THOSE ILLUSTRATED IN AR 220-45?
A: Yes. As long as they comply with the spirit and intent of this regulation.

14. Q: HOW ARE NAMES AND RANKS PLACED ON A DA FORM 6?
A: All names will be entered alphabetically within pay grade beginning with the highest pay grade.

15. Q: WHAT LETTER WILL INDICATE THOSE PERSONS NOT AVAILABLE BECAUSE OF BEING ABSENT WITHOUT LEAVE, IN ARREST, IN CONFINEMENT, SICK NOT IN THE LINE OF DUTY, OR OTHERWISE NOT AVAILABLE AS A RESULT OF THEIR OWN MISCONDUCT?
A: "U" -Unauthorized absence.

16. Q: TO WHAT ARMY COMPONENTS DOES AR 220-45 APPLY?
A: Active Army, Army Reserve, Army National Guard when in an inactive duty

training or annual training.

17. Q: WHEN MAY A PERSON'S NAME BE DELETED FROM THE DUTY ROSTER?
A: Whenever a person is excused from or not qualified to perform the duty concerned.

18. Q: FOR HOW MANY DAYS WILL A DUTY ROSTER BE POSTED?
A: Only for those days on which a detail is selected.

19. Q: WHEN THE ABBREVIATION "A" IS USED, WHAT WILL HAPPEN TO THE NUMBERING SEQUENCE OF DAYS OFF?
A: They will be interrupted.

20. Q: WHEN THE ABBREVIATION "D" OR "U" ARE USED, HOW IS THE NUMBERING SEQUENCE OF DAYS OFF WORK?
A: They will continue and the appropriate number will be included with the abbreviation.

21. Q: "H" IS EMPHASIZED THAT CO'S MAY USE WHATEVER SYSTEM BEST MEETS THEIR NEEDS AS LONG AS WHAT?
A: As long as equity is maintained.

Military Sanitation

1. Q: WHAT ARE THE THREE TYPES OF GERMS THAT FLIES MAY CARRY?
A: Typhoid
   Cholera
   Dysentery

2. Q: WHAT IS A VECTOR?
A: A carrier of disease (fly, flea, mosquito, ant).

3. Q: WHAT IS THE DIFFERENCE BETWEEN POTABLE WATER AND PALATABLE WATER?
A: "Potable water," is fit to drink. Palatable water is pleasing to the taste but

not necessarily fit to drink.

4. Q: WHAT DO YOU CALL THE LATRINE USED BY A SOLDIER ON THE MARCH?
A: A cat hole. (One foot square).

5. Q: WHO ARE THE INDIVIDUALS CHIEFLY RESPONSIBLE FOR THE HEALTH OF THE COMMAND?
A: Commander.
   Unit surgeon.

6. Q: WHO IS RESPONSIBLE FOR SANITATION IN THE FIELD?
A: The individual soldier.

7. Q: DEFINE "COMMUNICABLE DISEASES."
A: Communicable diseases are those illnesses which can be transmitted from man to man or from animal to man.

8. Q: WHAT IS SANITATION?
A: Sanitation is the effective use of measures which will create and maintain healthful environmental conditions.

9. Q: HOW FAR FROM THE NEAREST MESS FACILITY SHOULD A FIELD LATRINE BE BUILT?
A: At least 100 meters.

10. Q: WHAT TYPE OF DISEASE MIGHT YOU EXPECT TO GET IF YOU USED A DIRTY MESS KIT OR DRANK NONPOTABLE WATER?
A: Intestinal disease (dysentery).

11. Q: WHAT THREE WAYS MAY WATER BE PURIFIED UNDER FIELD CONDITIONS?
A: Boiling for 15 seconds. (A steady, rolling boil).
   Iodine tablets. One per quart of water (2 if water is cloudy). Insure the Iodine tablets are steel grey in color and are not crumbly.
   Calcium Hypochlorite ampules. 1/2 capful per canteen.

12. Q: WHEN SHOULD A TRENCH LATRINE BE ABANDONED?
A: When it is filled to within one foot of the surface.

13. Q: NAME TWO TYPES OF WATER WHICH SHOULD BE PURIFIED BY MEANS OF TWO IODINE TABLETS IN ONE QUART OF WATER.
A: Very cold water.
   Turbid water.
   Colored water.

14. Q: WHAT ARE THE DIMENSIONS OF A STRADDLE TRENCH?
A: Four feet long, one foot wide, 2 1/2 feet deep.

Army Emergency Relief

1. **Q: WHAT DOES THE ACRONYM <u>AER</u> STAND FOR?**
A: Army Emergency Relief.

2. **Q: AER PROVIDES FINANCIAL ASSISTANCE TO WHOM?**
A: Military personnel and their dependants.

3. **Q: HOW WILL LOANS TO THE ACTIVE DUTY PERSONNEL BE REPAID?**
A: By allotments.

4. **Q: WHO HAS OVERALL RESPONSIBILITY FOR UNIT AER PROGRAMS?**
A: Unit Commanders.

5. **Q: CAN AN ACTIVE DUTY STAFF SERGEANT IN THE UNITED STATES ARMY SERVE AS AN ASSISTANT AER OFFICER?**
A: Yes.

6. **Q: ARE RETIRED ARMY MEMBERS AUTHORIZED "AER" ASSISTANCE?**
A: Yes.

7. **Q: WHAT IS THE INTEREST RATE ON "AER" LOANS?**
A: None- AER does not charge any interest.

8. **Q: IS AER A PROFIT OR NONPROFIT ORGANIZATION?**
A: Nonprofit.

9. **Q: AER GIVES COMMANDERS AN IMPORTANT ASSET. WHAT DOES IT HELP THEM DO?**
A: Accomplish their basic command responsibility for the morale and welfare of Army members.

10. Q: ARE MEMBERS OF THE RESERVE COMPONENTS OF THE ARMY (ARMY NATIONAL GUARD AND U.S. ARMY RESERVE AUTHORIZED ASSISTANCE UNDER THE ARMY RELIEF PROGRAM?
A: Yes, if they have been on continuous active duty for more than 30 days.

11. Q: WHAT FORMS OF EMERGENCY RELIEF ASSISTANCE DOES AER PROVIDE?
A: a) Loan (interest free)
b) Grant (normally provided when it is found that repayment would cause undue hardship)
c) Combination loan and grant (used when partial repayment of the loan is possible)

12. Q: AER ASSISTANCE TO SPOUSES AND ORPHANS USUALLY OCCURS AT THE TIME OF, OR SHORTLY AFTER, DEATH OF THE ARMY MEMBER. IN WHAT FORM IS THIS ASSISTANCE NORMALLY PROVIDED?
A: In the form of a grant.

13. Q: IS IT POSSIBLE FOR SPOUSES AND ORPHANS WHO HAVE A CONTINUING SITUATION OF INADEQUATE INCOME TO MEET BASIC NEEDS TO RECEIVE A MONTHLY ALLOWANCE TO SUPPLEMENT THEIR INCOME?
A: Yes, but not for more than six months.

14. Q: WHAT TYPE OF SPECIAL ASSISTANCE MAY BE GIVEN?
A: Dental care, dentures, eyeglasses, hearing aids, wheelchairs, etc., and for amounts due for medical treatment after payments.

15. Q: WHAT FORMS OF ASSISTANCE MAY BE PROVIDED TO UNMARRIED DEPENDENT CHILDREN OF ARMY MEMBERS WHO NEED FINANCIAL ASSISTANCE?
A: Loans and scholarships.

16. Q: IF A LOAN IS MADE TO A DEPENDENT, WHO IS RESPONSIBLE FOR REPAYMENT OF THE LOAN?
A: The Army member.

17. Q: NAME THREE SITUATIONS FOR WHICH AER ASSISTANCE IS NOT AUTHORIZED.
A: a) Divorces
b) Marriages
c) Ordinary leave or vacations, etc.

18. Q: WHAT ARE SOME OF THE REASONS FOR WHICH AER ASSISTANCE IS AUTHORIZED?
A: a) Security deposit and first month's rent.
b) Emergency travel.
c) Non receipt of pay.

19. Q: IF THE PARENT OF AN ARMY MEMBER DIES AND THE ARMY MEMBER IS EXPECTED TO PAY THE FUNERAL COSTS (OR PART OF), IS AER ASSISTANCE AUTHORIZED TO THE SERVICE MEMBER?
A: Yes.

General Questions
Multiple References

1. Q: NAME THE RANKS OF "FIELD GRADE OFFICERS."
A: Colonel, Lieutenant Colonel, Major.

2. Q: WHAT ARE THE THREE BRANCHES OF THE UNITED STATES GOVERNMENT?
A: Executive.
   Judicial.
   Legislative.

3. Q: WHAT DO THE LETTERS "AER" STAND FOR?
A: Army Emergency Relief.

4. Q: ARMY EMERGENCY RELIEF LOANS ARE TO BE USED FOR WHAT PURPOSE?
A: To provide emergency financial assistance to Army members and their dependants.

5. Q: WHO IS THE SERGEANT MAJOR OF THE ARMY?
A: _____

6. Q: WHO IS COMMAND SERGEANT MAJOR OF YOUR BATTALION?
A: _____

7. Q: WHO IS RESPONSIBLE FOR SECURITY?
A: The individual soldier. (Everyone.)

8. Q: IS A PERSON ENTITLED TO WORSHIP AS (S)HE PLEASES UNDER THE GENEVA CONVENTION RULES?
A: Yes.

9. Q: WHO WAS THE FIRST GENERAL TO LEAD AN AMERICAN ARMY?
A: General George Washington.

10. Q: WHO IS THE DRUG AND ALCOHOL ABUSE CONTROL OFFICER FOR YOUR UNIT?
A: _____

11. Q: WHAT IS SUPPLY ECONOMY?
A: Making the best use of what supplies you have and requisitioning only what you need.

12. Q: WHAT BRANCH OF THE SERVICE IS THE OLDEST- ARMY, NAVY, OR AIR FORCE?
A: The U.S. Army (14 June 1775.)

13. Q: IS IT PROPER FOR A MALE SOLDIER TO CARRY AN UMBRELLA WHILE IN UNIFORM?
A: No.

14. Q: WHAT PRIVILEGE IS DENIED TO A MEMBER OF THE ARMED FORCES COMMITTED TO A MILITARY CONFINEMENT FACILITY?
A: Saluting.

15. Q: DOES THE PRESIDENT HAVE THE POWER TO DECLARE WAR AGAINST A NATION?
A: No. Only Congress can declare war.

16. Q: WHAT THREE NCO GRADES ARE NOT ADDRESSED AS SERGEANT?
A: Sergeants Major
   First Sergeant
   Corporal

17. Q: WHAT DO THE LETTERS "PMOS" REPRESENT?
A: Primary Military Occupation Speciality.

18. Q: HOW DOES THE ARMY EMERGENCY RELIEF OBTAIN FUNDS?
A: Only by voluntary contributions.

19. Q: WHAT DO THE LETTERS "ACS" REPRESENT?
A: Army Community Service.

20. Q: WHAT ARE THE THREE OPERATOR CHECKS FOR AN ARMY VEHICLE?
A: Before,
   During and

After operation.

21. Q: WHO IS AUTHORIZED TO GIVE A SOLDIER A FORMAL COUNSELING STATEMENT?
A: Unit Commander.

22. Q: WHAT IS "SAEDA"?
A: Subversion and Espionage Directed Against the U.S. Army.

23. Q: WHO IS THE COMMANDING OFFICER OF YOUR INSTALLATION?
A: _____

24. Q: WHO IS THE SECRETARY OF THE ARMY?
A: _____

25. Q: WHAT IS ORGANIZATIONAL EFFECTIVENESS?
A: A process that leads to treating people as human beings, to respect and consider, even if you don't agree with them. By processes such as communications, problem solving, coordination, decision making, goal setting and planning which are essential to mission accomplishment and combat readiness. The Army defines Organizational Effectiveness as the systematic military application of selected management and behavioral science skills and methods to improve how the total organization functions to accomplish assigned missions and increase combat readiness.

26. Q: IS IT TRUE THAT A SECURITY CLEARANCE ENTITLES AN INDIVIDUAL TO RECEIVE ALL INFORMATION CLASSIFIED UP TO AND INCLUDING THE DEGREE OF CLEARANCE WHICH (S)HE POSSESSES?
A: No.

27. Q: WHAT DOES "UCMJ" MEAN?
A: Uniform Code of Military Justice.

28. Q: WHAT TWO TYPES OF PATROLS ARE THERE?
A: Reconnaissance and Combat patrols.

29. Q: WHAT ARE THE THREE METHODS OF GIVING A CLASS?
A: Lecture.
   Demonstration.
   Conference.

30. Q: WHO WROTE THE NATIONAL ANTHEM AND WHEN?
A: Francis Scott Key. He was a prisoner aboard a British ship when the British were shelling Fort McHenry, Baltimore Harbor, Maryland, during the war of 1812. It was written in the year 1814.

31. Q: WHAT IS THE HIGHEST UNIFORMED POSITION WITHIN THE U.S.

ARMY?
A: The Chief of Staff of the Army.

32. Q: WHO IS THE ARMY CHIEF OF STAFF?
A: _____

33. Q: WHAT BUGLE CALL IS PLAYED FOR LIGHTS OUT?
A: Tatoo.

34. Q: WHO IS RESPONSIBLE FOR THE OVERALL SECURITY OF TROOPS IN A BIVOUAC AREA?
A: The senior commander of the units in the bivouac area.

35. Q: HOW CAN AN OBJECT BE SEEN BEST IN THE DARK?
A: By looking to either side or above or below the object.

36. Q: WHO PERFORMS FIRST ECHELON MAINTENANCE?
A: The user or the operator of the equipment.

37. Q: NAME FOUR OF THE TECHNICAL SERVICES?
A: Chemical
Signal
Transportation
Quartermaster
Ordnance
Medical
Engineer

38. Q: WHAT DOES "EEI" REPRESENT?
A: Essential Elements of Information.

39. Q: WHAT IS THE SMALLEST SELF SUPPORTING COMBAT UNIT?
A: A division.

40. Q: WHEN WALKING WITH A PERSON OF SENIOR GRADE YOU SHOULD ALWAYS WALK TO THAT INDIVIDUAL'S LEFT. WHY IS THIS?
A: In ancient times when armies met and were deployed in lines, the strongest warrior was placed on the right side and this was considered a position of honor.

41. Q: WHAT IS A MINE?
A: An encased charge of explosives fitted with a detonation device which may be set off by either vehicles or personnel.

42. Q: MINE DANGERS SIGNS ARE PAINTED IN WHAT COLORS?
A: Red.

43. Q: IF CAPTURED BY THE ENEMY DURING WARTIME, WHAT INFORMATION DO YOU PROVIDE?
A: Name.
　　Rank.
　　Serial Number (Social Security Accounting Number.)
　　Date of Birth.

44. Q: CAN A PRISONER OF WAR BE DEPRIVED OF HIS RANK?
A: No.

45. Q: WHAT IS THE ORIGIN OF THE SALUTE?
A: In early Roman history, persons meeting would raise their hand in the air, palm forward, to show they held no weapons and were therefore friendly. This has evolved into the present day salute.

47. Q: DEFINE THE WORDS "COVER" AND "CONCEALMENT" AS THEY RELATE TO MILITARY OPERATIONS.
A: Cover- Protection from hostile weapons.
　　Concealment- Protection from observation.

48. Q: FOR CEREMONIAL FIRING, HOW MANY MEN ARE IN THE FIRING SQUAD?
A: Seven soldiers and one NCO.

49. Q: NAME AT LEAST THREE INSECTS THAT CARRY DISEASE GERMS AND ONE DISEASE THAT EACH CARRY.
A: Mosquito...Malaria, Dinge Fever, Yellow Fever and Brain Fever.
　　Louse.............Typhus and Tench Fever.
　　Housefly.......Typhoid, Cholera and Dysentery.
　　Ticks..............Rocky Mountain, Rabbit and "Q" Fever.
　　Fleas...............Bubonic Plague and Typhus.
　　Mites...............Rickettsial Pox and Scabies.

50. Q: NAME THE FOUR ITEMS PLACED ON THE IDENTIFICATION TAG (DOG TAG.)
A: Name.
　　Social Security Accounting Number.
　　Blood type.
　　Religion.

51. Q: WHAT IS THE DIFFERENCE BETWEEN THE TERMS "FORT" AND "CAMP"?
A: Fort is permanent.
　　Camp is temporary.

**52. Q: COMMUNICATIONS ARE VERY IMPORTANT TO AN ARMY OPERATION IN THE FIELD. SOME OF THE MEANS OF COMMUNICATION

ARE: RADIO, TELEPHONE, AND MESSENGER. WHICH OF THESE IS THE MOST SECURE MEANS FROM ENEMY INTERCEPTION?
A: Messenger.

53. Q: WHEN WAS THE MEDAL OF HONOR APPROVED BY CONGRESS?
A: In the year 1862.

54. Q: WHEN CAPTURING A PRISONER OF WAR, THERE ARE FIVE THINGS YOU MUST REMEMBER. THEY ARE UNOFFICIALLY REFERRED TO AS THE FIVE "S". WHAT ARE THEY?
A: Search
Segregate
Silence
Speed
Safeguard

55. Q: WHAT MONETARY COMPENSATION ARE WINNERS OF THE MEDAL OF HONOR ENTITLED TO?
A: $100 per month for life.

56. Q: WHAT IS THE DA FORM 2A?
A: The Armed Forces Identification Card.

57. Q: WHAT INSIGNIA OF RANK DOES THE SERGEANT MAJOR OF THE ARMY WEAR?
A: Three stripes up and three down with two stars in the center. It is similar to the Sergeant Major insignia of rank, but instead of one star it has two.

58. Q: RECITE YOUR THREE GENERAL ORDERS.
A: I will guard everything within the limits of my post and quit my post only when properly relieved.
 I will obey my special orders and perform all my duties in a military manner.
 I will report violations of my special orders, emergencies, and anything not covered in my instructions to the Commander of the relief.

59. Q: WHO IS YOUR COMPANY COMMANDER?
A: _____

60. Q: WHO IS YOUR COMPANY FIRST SERGEANT?
A: _____

61. Q: WHAT MILITARY LEADER DEMANDED "SEND ME MEN WHO CAN SHOOT AND SALUTE"?
A: General John J. Pershing- in the First World War.

62. Q: WHO SAID "I SHALL RETURN", AND WHERE WAS HE WHEN HE

SAID IT?
A: General Douglas MacArthur in the Philippines.

63. Q: CAN AN "AER" LOAN BE USED TO ACCOMPLISH REPAIR ON A PRIVATELY OWNED VEHICLE?
A: Yes- providing the vehicle is considered essential to unit mission, for commuting to and from duty station when other transportation is unavailable, or for transportation of an ill dependent.

64. Q: NAME THREE PEOPLE WHO HAVE HELD THE RANK OF GENERAL OF THE ARMY?
A: George G. Marshall
   Dwight D. Eisenhower.
   Omar Bradley.
   Douglas MacArthur.

65. Q: WHAT IS THE MAIN PURPOSE OF THE GENEVA CONVENTION RULES COVERING THE TREATMENT OF PRISONERS?
A: In general, the rules provide that prisoners must be treated humanely. Specifically forbidden are "violence to life and person — cruel treatment and torture — outrages on personal dignity." In particular, humiliating and degrading treatment.

66. Q: IS THE "SGLI" (SERVICEMEN'S GROUP LIFE INSURANCE) PROGRAM MANDATORY FOR ALL SOLDIERS?
A No. Participation is strictly voluntary.

67. Q: WHAT ARE THE FOUR TYPES OF INSPECTIONS?
A: In ranks
   Quarters
   Full field
   Show down

68. Q: AS A COMBAT OR COMBAT SUPPORT SOLDIER, YOU MAY BE REQUIRED TO REPORT ENEMY ACTIVITIES IN THE BATTLEFIELD. THE CODEWORD "SALUTE" WILL HELP YOU TO GATHER AND REPORT INFORMATION ABOUT THE ENEMY. WHAT DOES THE WORD "SALUTE" REPRESENT?
A: S - Size of the enemy unit (squad, platoon, company.)
   A - Activity of the enemy (What are they doing?)
   L - Location of the enemy (Where are they?)
   U - Unit of the enemy (Infantry, ground troops, etc.)
   T - Time you observed the enemy.
   E - Equipment the enemy is carrying or using.

69. Q: WHAT DOES OPERATOR'S MAINTENANCE CONSIST OF?
A: An inspector to determine if items are in good condition, correctly as-

sembled, not excessively worn, not leaking and adequately lubricated.

70. Q: HOW IS INFORMATION PASSED TO MILITARY PERSONNEL?
A: Through use of the Chain of Command.

71. Q: CAN THREE CIVILIANS RATE, INDORSE AND REVIEW A SOLDIER ON A SINGLE EVALUATION REPORT?
A: No. At least one of the individuals must be military.

72. Q: WHAT ARE THE OBJECTIVES OF THE ARMY'S HUMAN RELATIONS AND EQUAL OPPORTUNITY PROGRAM?
A: To provide equality of opportunity, eliminate discrimination and achieve racial harmony.

73. Q: WHAT IS THE DEFINITION OF PERSONAL RACISM OR SEXISM?
A: The acting out of prejudices by individuals against other individuals or groups, because of race or gender.

The Army Maintenance Management System

1. Q: WHAT IS DA PAM 738-750?
A: The Army Maintenance Management System.

2. Q: WHAT IS DA FORM 1970?
A: Motor Vehicle Utilization Record.

3. Q: WHAT IS DA FORM 2402?
A: Exchange tag.

4. Q: WHAT IS DD FORM 314?
A: Preventive Maintenance Schedule and Record.

5. Q: WHAT IS DA FROM 2405?
A: Maintenance Request Register.

6. Q: WHAT IS DA FROM 2407?

A: Maintenance Request.

7. Q: WHAT IS DA FORM 2406?
A: Material Condition Status Report.

8. Q: WHAT IS DA FORM 2408-5?
A: Equipment Modification Record.

9. Q: WHAT IS DA FORM 2408-9?
A: Equipment Control Record.

10. Q: WHAT IS DA FORM 2408-10?
A: Equipment Component Register.

11. Q: WHAT IS DA FORM 2408-17?
A: Uncorrected Fault Record.

12. Q: WHAT IS DA FORM 2401?
A: This gives a ready record as to the user and location of equipment while on dispatch or in use, know as Organization Control Record for Equipment.

13. Q: WHAT IS THE PURPOSE FOR DD FORM 314?
A: This form supplies the means of recording scheduled and performed organizational maintenance, lubrication services, oil sampling and recording nonavailable time.

14. Q: WHAT IS NMCS/NMCM?
A: NMCS- Not Mission Capable Study.
   NMCM- Not Mission Capable Maintenance.

15. Q: WHAT DETERMINES NMC (NOT MISSION CAPABLE)?
A: Equipment is not mission capable or not ready when it cannot perform its combat missions.

16. Q: ON WHAT FORM IS NMC/NMCS POSTED?
A: DD Form 314.

17. Q: WHAT IS DA FORM 2404 USED FOR?
A: DA Form 2404 is used for recording equipment faults found during the operations inspection.

18. Q: WHO USES DA FORM 2404?
A: DA Form 2404 will be used by all personnel performing inspections, maintenance services, diagnostic checkouts and technical evaluations.

19. Q: WHEN IS DA FORM 2408-1 USED?
A: This form is used when a DD Form 1970 is not issued to authorize use of

equipment.

20. Q: WHAT FOUR ITEMS ARE POSTED DAILY ON DA FORM 2808-1?
A: Hours, miles, fuel, oil.

21. Q: WHAT IS DA FORM 2408-4?
A: Weapon Record Data.

22. Q: WHAT IS DA FORM 2408-4 USED FOR?
A: This form is used to record firings and other information related to the service life of weapons with cannon or mortar tubes.

23. Q: WHAT IS DA FORM 2408-5?
A: Equipment Modification Record.

24. Q: WHAT IS THE PURPOSE FOR DA FORM 2408-5?
A: This form records the requirements for and application of modifications of missile systems and selected missile components.

25. Q: WHAT IS THE PURPOSE FOR DA FORM 2408-14?
A: This form is a record of uncorrected faults on equipment.

26. Q: WHAT IS THE PURPOSE FOR DA FORM 2409?
A: Equipment Maintenance Log (consolidated) record provides a complete maintenance history of an item of equipment.

27. Q: WHAT IS THE PURPOSE FOR DA FORM 1970 (MOTOR VEHICLE UTILIZATION RECORD)?
A: This form supplies a record for the control of equipment usage.

28. Q: WHAT FORM MAY REPLACE DD FORM 1970 WHEN AUTHORIZED BY THE COMMANDERS?
A: DA Form 2408-1 (Equipment Daily Log).

29. Q: WHAT IS THE PURPOSE FOR DA FORM 2401 (ORGANIZATION CONTROL RECORD FOR EQUIPMENT)?
A: The form gives a ready record as to the user and location of equipment while on dispatch or in use.

30. Q: WHO IS RESPONSIBLE FOR INITIATING DA FORM 1970?
A: The dispatcher.

31. Q: WHAT IS DA FORM 2408-20?
A: Oil Analysis Log.

32. Q: WHAT IS THE PURPOSE OF DA FORM 2408-20?
A: This form supplies a record of oil samples taken and the results of labora-

tory analysis.

33. Q: WHAT IS DA FORM 2408-18?
A: Equipment Inspection List.

34. Q: WHAT IS THE DA FORM 2408-18 USED FOR?
A: This form gives a list of all required inspections of equipment which are not listed on other TAMMS forms.

35. Q: WHAT IS DA FORM 2416 USED FOR?
A: DA Form 2416 is used to schedule, record, and report calibration services.

36. Q: WHAT IS DA FORM 2417?
A: U.S. Army Calibration System Rejected Instrument.

37. Q: WHEN IS DA FORM 2417 USED?
A: When an instrument cannot be calibrated to the required accuracy.

38. Q: IF NO FAULTS ARE FOUND ON A PIECE OF EQUIPMENT, WHAT ACTION WOULD BE TAKEN ON DA FORM 2404?
A: Enter the date and initial DA Form 2404.

39. Q: WHAT THREE TYPES OF CHECKS ARE THERE FOR BASIC USE OF DA FORM 2404?
A: Before, during, and after operations.

40. Q: ARE THERE OTHER USES OF DA FORM 2405 BY A COMMAND?
A: This form may be used as a reference for answering inquiries pertaining to a specific maintenance request, or as a source of data for information and reports desired by all levels of command, such as backlog, job status, etc.

Command and Other Channels

Chain of Command
Commander-in-Chief
Secretary of Defense
Secretary of the Army
Chief of Staff of the Army
Commanding General
Installation Commander
Brigade Commander
Battalion Commander
Company Commander
Platoon Leader

NCO Support Channels
Sergeant Major of the Army
Command Sergeant Major, Bde
Command Sergeant Major, Bn
YOUR NCO CHAIN
1._____
2._____
3._____
4._____
5._____
6._____

Equal Opportunity

1. Q: THE U.S. ARMY RACE RELATION AND EQUAL OPPORTUNITY PROGRAM HAS THREE OBJECTIVES. WHAT ARE THEY?
A: To provide equality of opportunity, eliminate discrimination and achieve racial harmony.

2. Q: WHAT ARE SOME OF THE RESPONSIBILITIES OF INSTALLATION COMMANDERS FOR ON-POST/OFF-POST?
A: All on-post facilities and official activities must be open, as appropriate, to all DOD personnel and dependents regardless of race, color, religion, sex, age or national origin.

3. Q: WHAT IS THE DEPARTMENT OF THE ARMY POLICY ON DEPENDENT AND CIVILIAN SCHOOLS?
A: DA policy supports the right of dependent children of military personnel to be assigned to, and attend, public schools on a nondiscriminatory basis.

4. Q: WHAT IS THE DEFINITION OF EQUAL OPPORTUNITY?
A: Equal opportunity, as used in this directive, means equal consideration and treatment based upon merit, fitness and capability.

5. Q: WHAT IS THE DEFINITION OF ETHNIC GROUP?
A: A group of individuals distinguished from the general population based on actual or perceived cultural criteria (language, life style, religion, or national origin).

6. Q: WHAT IS A MINORITY GROUP?
A: Any group distinguished from the general population in terms of race, religion, sex, age or national origin.

7. Q: NAME THE FOUR SPECIFIC LEARNING OBJECTIVES OF UNIT EO

TRAINING.
A: 1) To facilitate and improve the soldier's understanding of the entire equal opportunity program for the United States Army.
    2) To inform unit members about potential sources of minority/gender dissatisfaction and interracial/intersexual tension in the Army.
    3) To increase the soldiers understanding and acceptance of different cultural modes.
    4) To provide the chain of command with contemporary information and feedback on the status and progress and the equal opportunity program.

8. Q: WHAT DOES AAP MEAN?
A: Affirmative Actions Plan.

9. Q: WHAT ARE SOME SPECIFIC AAP OBJECTIVES?
A: 1) Eliminate discrimination.
    2) Achieve racial harmony.
    3) Ensure effective implementation of command policy and programs.
    4) Develop positive subprograms and projects designed to ensure equality of opportunity for all military and civilian personnel.
    5) Orient each member of the command regarding command Race Relations and Equal Opportunity (RR/EO) Programs.

10. Q: WHAT IS THE PRIMARY CHANNEL FOR CORRECTING DISCRIMINATORY PRACTICE?
A: The Chain of Command.

11. Q: THE EO PROGRAM HAS TWO EQUAL AND COMPLEMENTARY COMPONENTS. WHAT ARE THEY?
A: 1) The affirmative actions component.
    2) The education and training component.

12. Q: WHAT AR IS USED BY COMMANDERS FOR PROCESSING COMPLAINTS?
A: AR 20-1.

13. Q: WHEN IS FORMAL TRAINING ON EO/RR FIRST GIVEN?
A: During BCT/BT, and for all newly commissioned officers during OBC.

14. Q: BY WHOM WILL THE MINIMUM UNIT EO TRAINING REQUIREMENTS BE SPECIFIED?
A: MACOC (Major Army Command).

15. Q: WHERE WILL THE EO OFFICE BE LOCATED?
A: Within the organizational structure where it can be most effective.

16. Q: WHO IS THE PRINCIPAL ASSISTANT TO THE COMMANDER IN THE DEVELOPMENT AND SUPERVISION OF EO MATTERS.

A: The EO staff officer.

17. Q: WHO INVESTIGATES ALLEGATIONS OF DISCRIMINATION IN OFF-POST HOUSING?
A: Housing Referral Officer.

18. Q: WHAT DOES DRRI MEAN?
A: Defense Race Relation Institute.

19. Q: WHAT MOS DO ENLISTED PERSONNEL WORKING IN THE RACE RELATIONS/EQUAL OPPORTUNITY PROGRAM HAVE?
A: OOU.

20. Q: AT WHAT LEVELS WILL RR/EO COUNCILS BE ESTABLISHED?
A: Brigade, Community, battalion and equivalent level commands.

21. Q: WHEN WAS THE PRIVACY ACT INTRODUCED?
A: 1974.

22. Q: WHAT AR DEALS WITH THE EQUAL OPPORTUNITY PROGRAM IN THE ARMY?
A: AR 600-21.

23. Q: WHERE WILL FORMAL EDUCATION FOR EO/RR OF NCO'S AND OFFICERS BE GIVEN?
A: NCO'S, NCO Academy, Officer's advanced courses and the Command and General Staff College.

24. Q: WHO WILL GIVE FORMAL INSTRUCTION AT THE SERGEANTS MAJOR ACADEMY, ARMY WAR COLLEGE?
A: The senior officer/enlisted personnel.

25. Q: WHAT IS THE DEFINITION OF PERSONAL RACISM (SEXISM)?
A: The acting out of prejudices by individuals against other individuals or groups, because of race or gender.

26. Q: WHO HAS THE RIGHT TO DESIGNATE A PRIVATELY-OWNED ESTABLISHMENT AS OFF-LIMITS?
A: Commanders.

27. Q: IF YOU WERE DISCRIMINATED AGAINST ON HOUSING TO WHOM WOULD YOU GO TO SEEK HELP?
A: Your commander.

28. Q: WHEN WILL EO/RR TRAINING NOT BE HELD IN SMALL GROUPS?
A: Field trips, or when the presentation of factual material deems open discussion among group members as inappropriate.

30. Q: WHAT APPENDIX OF AR 600-21 DEALS WITH GUIDELINES FOR UNIT TRAINING?
A: Appendix D.

31. Q: WHAT CHAPTER OF AR 600-21 DEALS WITH EDUCATION AND TRAINING?
A: Chapter 3.

32. Q: WHAT IS THE EQUAL OPPORTUNITY PROGRAM?
A: A single program with two equal and complementary components.

33. Q: WHAT DOES AFFIRMATIVE ACTIONS CONSIST OF?
A: It consists of a series of initiatives aggressively pursued to search out areas of inequity and discrimination to take corrective action.

34. Q: WHAT IS THE EDUCATION AND TRAINING COMPONENT?
A: It is a continuing Army-wide effort to impart to all members of the Army an awareness concerning equal opportunity matters, to develop positive attitudes toward the program, and to foster good relationships among individuals and groups.

35. Q: WHO IS RESPONSIBLE FOR CONDUCTING EO TRAINING ON A CONTINUAL BASIS FOR COMMANDER, KEY CIVILIAN AND MILITARY STAFF PERSONNEL?
A: All commanders and supervisors.

36. Q: HOW WILL THE PROCEDURES FOR PROCESSING COMPLAINTS BE POSTED?
A: They will be in writing and will be displayed prominently on a permanent basis where all unit members will have open access to them.

37. Q: WHO HANDLES COMPLAINTS UNDER THE AFFIRMATIVE ACTIONS PLAN?
A: The commander will rely on the appropriate staff agencies to aid in handling complaints and grievances. When appropriate, an independent investigator should be appointed.

38. Q: WILL THE ARMY PAY FOR EDUCATION AT AN INSTITUTION THAT UNLAWFULLY DISCRIMINATES IN THE ADMISSION OF STUDENTS?
A: No.

39. Q: WHAT AR PROVIDES ARMY POLICIES AND PROCEDURES REGARDING EQUAL OPPORTUNITY IN OFF-POST HOUSING?
A: AR 600-18.

40. Q: WHAT STATEMENT MUST BE INCLUDED ON MILITARY ORDERS?

A: You are required to report to the family housing or housing referral officer serving your new duty station before making housing arrangements for renting, leasing or purchasing off-post housing.

41. Q: WHAT IS THE OBJECTIVE OF EQUAL OPPORTUNITY EDUCATION?
A: To promote equal opportunity by developing maximum potential of all available talents and resources.

42. Q: WHAT WILL EO INSTRUCTIONS FOCUS ON?
A: Interpersonal relations, the impact of institutional discrimination, equality of opportunity, and contemporary factors influencing unit harmony, effectiveness, and mission accomplishment.

43. Q: WHAT WILL UNIT TRAINING ON EO CONSIST OF?
A: Informing unit members of policies and activities concerning equal opportunity.

44. Q: WHAT DO THE LETTERS UDL STAND FOR?
A: Unit Discussion Leader.

45. Q: WHAT CHAPTER OF AR 600-21 DEALS WITH AFFIRMATIVE ACTIONS?
A: Chapter 2.

46. Q: WHAT APPENDIX OF AR 600-21 GIVES EXPLANATION OF TERMS?
A: Appendix A.

47. Q: WHAT IS THE DEFINITION OF HOUSING DISCRIMINATION?
A: The act of denying housing to Army personnel because of race, color, religion, sex, age, or national origin.

48. Q: WHAT ARE RESTRICTIVE SANCTIONS?
A: Actions taken to preclude Army personnel from entering into a new rental or lease arrangement with an agent of a housing facility which has been found to have discriminated against military personnel.

49. Q: WHAT ARE THE PREREQUISITES OF PERSONNEL WHO ATTEND DRRI?
A: 1) Have demonstrated leadership attributes.
   2) Must have one year of service remaining after completion of course.
   3) Must not have traits of character which are questionable.

50. Q: WHAT APPENDIX DEALS WITH THE FORMAT FOR NARRATIVE AND STATISTICAL REPORTS?
A: Appendix C.

**51. Q: WHAT IS THE FORMAT FOR NARRATIVE AND STATISTICAL RE-

PORTS ON EO PROGRESS?
A: 1) General analysis of local conditions.
    2) Integration of minority groups and women throughout the various military organizational levels.
    3) Statistical analysis.
    4) Goals met or accomplished.
    5) Goals not met and why; planned actions.
    6) Community affairs.

Military Programs

ACS   ARMY COMMUNITY SERVICE

ACS is staffed by Army personnel, civilian employees, and community volunteers. Some of the services provided include:

1) Loan closet: household items made available for temporary loan.
2) Geographic file: file maintained on Army posts world-wide.
3) Welcome packets: general information about the installation and area.
4) Family counseling and referral services.
5) Exceptional Family Member program: lists programs and facilities available.
6) Citizenship instruction assistance.
7) Financial planning and Budget counseling.
8) Family Advocacy Program: spouse/child abuse, foster care, shelter aid.
9) Child Development Center: Day-Care nursery, Pre-kindergarten.
10) AER: Army Emergency Relief (see AER).
11) EERC: Employment opportunity assistance for military spouse and family members.

AER   ARMY EMERGENCY RELIEF

In an emergency situation and when AER assistance is needed, the service member should see the unit Commander or the nearest AER office. Services provided include:

1) Financial assistance for valid emergency needs such as:

        food
        rent
        required travel
        utilities
        essential car
        medical bills

essential dental care
funeral expenses
essential needs when pay not received or funds lost

2) Assistance in the form of interest-free loans; may be an outright grant when loan repayment would cause undue hardship.

3) Education assistance for undergraduate study by dependent children of military personnel.

EERC   EDUCATION AND EMPLOYMENT RESOURCE CENTER

Services available through EERC include:

1) Seminars on resume' writing, the interview process, searching the job market.
2) Seminars on understanding the Federal Employment system, filling out the SF 171.
3) Counseling, information and referral on employment opportunities.
4) Job bank of positions available in the area and on the installation.

RED CROSS

Services of the American Red Cross available to Armed Forces personnel, veterans, and their family members include:

1) Assistance in emergency situations; assisting service members and their families to meet basic maintenance and emergency needs.

2) Providing communications through Red Cross channels between military personnel and family members concerning health and welfare matters.

3) Provide information in decisions involving compassionate reassignment and dependency discharge.

4) Assistance regarding emergency leave.

5) Assist families in establishing their eligibility for financial, medical, and other government benefits.

6) Provide financial assistance in a grant or loan.

7) Provide referral service to agencies in legal aid, medical or psychiatric care, employment, or family or children's welfare.

8) Giving help and counsel in relation to personal and family problems that arise during military service.

9) Provide disaster health services.

10) Provide training/certification programs for Red Cross volunteers.

11) Plan and provide recreation services in voluntary off-duty activities.

12) Supervise trained Red Cross volunteers who provide personal services and assistance to medical facility patients and staff.

13) Provide training classes and certification in:
    a. First Aid and CPR
    b. Boating Safety
    c. Lifesaving and Water Safety
    d. Parenthood Preparation
    e. Babysitting Course

EO   EQUAL OPPORTUNITY

The Equal Opportunity (EO) Program is designed to:

1) Provide EO for military personnel and their family members both on and off-post, including on and off-post housing.

2) Provide equal opportunity and treatment for uniformed members and their families irrespective of race, color, religion, sex, or national origin except as necessary to support established affirmative action goals.

3) Insure fair treatment for all soldiers based solely on merit, fitness, capability, and potential.

4) Insure that soldiers will not be accessed, classified, trained, assigned, promoted, or otherwise managed on the basis of race, color, religion, sex, or national origin.

CHAMPUS   CIVILIAN HEALTH AND MEDICAL PROGRAMS OF THE UNIFORMED SERVICE

1) CHAMPUS is a health benefits program that provides for authorized inpatient and outpatient care from civilian sources on a cost-sharing basis. Persons eligible for CHAMPUS: 1) active duty dependents and retired military and their family members, and 2) family members of deceased active duty or retired military personnel.

2) For authorized out patient care, the patient is subject to a $50 deductible per person each fiscal year, up to a maximum of $100 per family. Of the remainder of the cost of care, the government will pay 80% of the allowable charges for active duty dependents and 75% of the allowable charges for retirees and their family members.

3) CHAMPUS users who live near a military hospital and who have civilian major medical insurance (i.e. Blue Cross, Blue Shield, etc) may now get supplemental coverage from CHAMPUS for non-emergency inpatient care without first requiring a nonavailability statement from the military facility. This new ruling makes it easier to get inpatient care from a civilian doctor or hospital.

a. Personnel who live within the zip code area of a military hospital are required to go to that hospital for non-emergency inpatient care. CHAMPUS eligibles should ensure that they are eligible before securing care under the CHAMPUS program. A non availability statement may be insured for CHAMPUS coverage only when the inpatient medical care is not available at a military facility.

PRIMUS   PRIMARY MEDICAL CARE FOR UNIFORMED SERVICE

A new approach to providing military beneficiaries ready access to primary health care.
Open 365 days per year.
Open 0700 to 2000 hours weekdays.
    0700 to 1400 hours weekend and holidays.
No appointment necessary.
No cost to eligible patients for treatment or pharmaceuticals.
Services will be provided to all entitled to care at military treatment facilities, including all active and retired uniformed services personnel and their dependents.
Basic laboratory and pharmacy services are provided on-site.
Licensed and credentialed physicians and staff will provide services.
Primary care physicians will treat patients on a walk-in-basis.
Location: 3031 Javier Road, Fairfax, VA.
Services provide by PHP Corporation, Falls Church, Virginia.

ADAPCP   ALCOHOL AND DRUG ABUSE PREVENTION AND CONTROL PROGRAM

1) ADACP provides assistance for all alcohol and drug problems.

2) Any incident involving alcohol or drugs makes it mandatory for active duty military to be evaluated.

3) Soldiers identified as alcohol or other drug abusers who do not warrant retention will be processed for separation from the military.

4) Soldiers identified as alcohol or other drug abusers who, in the opinion of their commanders warrant retention, will be afforded the opportunity for rehabilitation through ADAPCP.

5) Active duty personnel enroll in the program through their unit; DOD civilians may come in to see a counselor to enroll.

AEC   ARMY EDUCATION CENTER

Services available through the Army Education Center include:

1) COUNSELING
    a. Educational counseling: academic/skill development/VOC Tech

    b. Tuition Benefits: VEAP, VA, Tuition Assistance.
    c. Army Apprenticeship Program
    d. Evaluation of military education for college credit.

2) TESTING
    a. High school examination program: GED.
    b. College level examinations: CLEP, DANTES, ACT-PEP, Placement.
    c. College admission: SAT, ACT, GMAT, GRE.
    d. Foreign languages: German Headstart, CLEP language exams.
    e. Military personnel exams: AFCT, OSB, FAST, DLAB, DLPT.
    f. Other: Interest Inventory, Aptitude, Achievement, Diagnostic, Basic Math and Science, BNCOC Test.

3) BSEP/BASIC SKILLS EDUCATION PROGRAM
    a. Basic skills/GT Improvement
    b. English-As-A-Second-Language

4) ASEP/ADVANCED SKILLS EDUCATION PROGRAM
    a. Supervision
    b. Management
    c. Communication

5) MOS IMPROVEMENT COURSES
    a. Effective Writing
    b. Preparation of Military Correspondence
    c. TAFFS/The Army Functional Files System
    d. Reading Management
    e. Standard English Grammar and Usage

6) ARMY LEARNING CENTER (ALC)
    a. Career Development Information
    b. MOS Library: TM, FM, AR, etc. available for checkout
    c. TEC Center: MOS related TEC tapes and lessons to view or checkout
    d. Exportable Training Courses: enrollment in Army, AF, USN, USMC, courses
    e. Foreign Language program (self study lab)

Earning Promotion Points Through Education

1) **Military Education**

a) Military Correspondence Courses: Soldiers earn one promotion point for every five credit hours of correspondence course completion. Points are not awarded for duplicate subcourses.

b) NCOES Courses: Some NCOES courses (except for ANCOC) may be completed by correspondence. Soldiers receive certificates for completion for the appropriate level of NCOES: E4/E5 earn one promotion point for every five credit hours of correspondence completed.

2) **Civilian Education**

a) Business/Trade School/College: Promotion points will be awarded for Business/Trade School and commercial correspondence courses from accredited schools. Sixteen (16) classroom hours is equivalent to a semester hour as documented on a completion certificate or transcript. Soldiers earn on point for each semester hour earned.

b) High School Diploma/GED: No points awarded.

c) Education Improvement: Ten points are awarded for completion of one of the following actions while on active duty:

   a. obtain a high school diploma/GED
   b. complete an accredited post secondary course (college level)
   c. Improvement of the GT Score

REFERENCE: AR 600-200, Enlisted Personnel management System (EPMS) Chapter 7, Promotions, in ENLISTED RANKS PERSONNEL UPDATE.

This Promotion Study Guide is not an official publication. Soldiers should study the topics included in the Guide, paying particular attention to the forms (DA 3355 and DA 3356) and utilizing referenced publications to prepare for the Promotion Board.

The Flag of the United States

AUTHORIZATION: The Flag of the United States is the symbol of our nation. The union, white stars on a field of blue, is the honor point of the flag, the right being the place of honor. The union of the flag, and the flag itself when in company with other flags, is always given the honor position, i.e., the marching right, the flag's own right, or an observer's left facing the flag.

TIME AND OCCASIONS FOR DISPLAY:
 a. The flag of the United States will be displayed outdoors at all Army installations.
 b. Only one flag of the United States will be flown at one time at any continental United States (CONUS) Army installation except as authorized by the commanding generals of major Army commands.
 c. The flag will be displayed daily from reveille to retreat. If illuminated, it may be displayed at night during special events or on special occasions deemed appropriate by the commander.
 d. The flag of the United States is the only flag which may be flown from a flagpole over an Army installation. An exception is the Minuteman flag which, if awarded, may be flown beneath the flag of the United States.
 e. In unusual circumstances not covered in Army regulations, the judgement of the senior Army individual present will be used to determine whether the flag shall be displayed on a specific occasion.

SIZES AND OCCASIONS FOR DISPLAY: National flags listed below are for outdoor display:
 a. Garrison flag: twenty feet hoist (height) by thirty-eight feet fly (length), of nylon-wool. The garrison flag is flown on holidays, as listed in AR 600-25, and other important occasions, as designated by Presidential proclamation.
 b. Post flag: 8 feet 11 3/8 inches hoist (height) by 17 feet fly (length), of nylon. The post flag is flown daily. When a garrison flag is not authorized, the post flag will be flown on holidays and important occasions.

c. Field flag: 6 feet 8 inches hoist (height) by 12 feet fly (length), of nylon-wool. The field flag is displayed with the positional field flag.
d. Storm flag: 5 feet hoist (height) by 9 feet 6 inches fly (length), of nylon. The storm flag is flown in inclement weather.

Code of Conduct

For members of the Armed Forces of the United States.

I
I am an American, fighting in the forces which guard my country and our way of life. I am prepared to give my life in their defense.

II
I will never surrender of my own free will. If in command I will never surrender the members of my command while they still have the means to resist.

III
If I am captured I will continue to resist by all means available. I will make every effort to escape and aid others to escape. I will accept neither parole nor special favors from the enemy.

IV
If I become prisoner of war, I will keep faith in my fellow prisoners. I will give no information or take part in any action which might be harmful to my comrades. If I am senior, I will take command. If not, I will obey the lawful orders of those appointed over me and will back them up in every way.

V
When questioned, should I become a prisoner of war, I am required to give name, rank, service, number, and date of birth. I will evade answering further questions to the utmost of my ability. I will make no oral or written statements disloyal to my country and its allies or harmful to their cause.

VI
I will never forget that I am an American, fighting for freedom, responsible for my actions, and dedicated to the principles which made my country free. I will trust in my God and in the United States of America.

1. Q: WHO DOES THE CODE OF CONDUCT APPLY TO?

A: To all members of the United States Armed Forces.

2. Q: WHEN DOES THE CODE OF CONDUCT APPLY TO ARMED FORCES PERSONNEL?

A: At all times.

3. Q: WHAT IS THE OBJECTIVE OF THE CODE OF CONDUCT?
A: To increase unit fighting strength and instill in the individual the responsibility to oppose hostile forces by all means available and to evade capture or surrender.

4. Q: WHAT IS THE MAIN RESPONSIBILITY OF AN INDIVIDUAL IF TAKEN AS A PRISONER OF WAR?
A: 1) Resist interrogations and indoctrination.
    2) Maintain loyalty with and assist fellow prisoners of war.
    3) Make every attempt to escape and help others to escape.

5. Q: WHY WAS THE CODE OF CONDUCT DEVELOPED?
A: To provide a form of mental defense for U.S. prisoners of war to use to resist illegal enemy prisoners of war management practices.

6. Q: THE CODE OF CONDUCT SUPPORTS THE INTENT OF THE GENEVA CONVENTION. WHY?
A: So that prisoners of war may not be used or forced to further the enemy war effort.

7. Q: WHAT IS THE RELATIONSHIP OF THE CODE OF CONDUCT TO THE UNIFORM CODE OF MILITARY JUSTICE (UCMJ)?
A: It is one of mutual support.

8. Q: WHAT PROVIDES THE LEGAL AUTHORITY TO SUPPORT THE CODE OF CONDUCT?
A: The Uniform code of Military Justice.

9. Q: WHO WOULD ASSUME COMMAND IN A PRISONER OF WAR CAMP?
A: The senior person eligible for command regardless of service, has an obligation to assume command.

10. Q: WHAT IS THE ONLY INFORMATION THAT A PRISONER OF WAR IS REQUIRED TO GIVE TO A CAPTAIN?
A: Name, rank, identification number and date of birth.

11. Q: WHAT SUPPORTS THE INTENT THAT PRISONERS OF WAR MAY NOT BE USED OR FORCED TO FURTHER THE ENEMY WAR EFFORT?
A: Code of Conduct.

12. Q: HOW HAS THE ENEMY OFTEN VIEWED PRISONERS OF WAR?
A: As valuable sources of military information and of propaganda which can be used to further the enemy's war effort.

**13. Q: WHAT CAN HAPPEN TO A PRISONER OF WAR IF HE SHOULD CON-

FER TO OR SIGN A STATEMENT HE MAKES TO AN ENEMY?
A: He can be convicted as a war criminal.

14. Q: WHAT SHOULD A PRISONER OF WAR DO IF HE HAS UNWILLINGLY OR ACCIDENTLY DISCLOSED INFORMATION TO THE ENEMY?
A: Regroup his thoughts and begin resistance again using a fresh approach or an alternative line of mental defense.

15. Q: THE CODE OF CONDUCT IS PRESCRIBED BY EXECUTIVE ORDER NUMBER 10631. WHAT YEAR WAS IT EFFECTIVE?
A: 17 August 1955.

16. Q: WHAT IS AN ENEMY STATE?
A: A state recognized or unrecognized which is at war with the United States or engaged in armed conflict with the United States.

17. Q: WHAT DOES AN INDIVIDUAL REMAIN ACCOUNTABLE FOR WHILE ISOLATED FROM FRIENDLY FORCES OR WHILE HELD BY THE ENEMY?
A: His actions.

18. Q: PRISONER OF WAR COMPOUNDS ARE IN MANY WAYS AN EXTENSION OF WHAT?
A: The battlefield.

19. Q: UNDER THE GENEVA CONVENTION, WHO ARE CONSIDERED RETAINED PERSONNEL AND NOT CONSIDERED PRISONERS OF WAR?
A: Medical personnel and chaplains.

20. Q: IF THE ENEMY WERE TO FOLLOW THE INTENT OF THE PROVISION OF THE GENEVA PRISONER OF WAR CONVENTION, WHAT WOULD HAPPEN TO SERIOUSLY SICK AND WOUNDED PRISONERS OF WAR?
A: They would be offered reparation as soon as their medical condition permits movement even during active hostilities.

21. Q: IT IS IMPORTANT THAT THE SENIOR PERSON IN A PRISONER OF WAR CAMP ESTABLISH WHAT?
A: Organization.

22. Q: THE SENIOR PERSONS IN A PRISONER OF WAR CAMP ARE OBLIGATED TO REPRESENT PRISONERS UNDER HIS SUPERVISION IN WHAT MATTERS?
A: Camp administration, health welfare, and grievances.

23. Q: IS A PRISONER OF WAR REQUIRED TO FILL OUT A GENEVA CONVENTION "CAPTURE CARD?"
A: No, it is allowed but not required.

24. Q: WHAT ARMY REGULATION GOVERNS CODE OF CONDUCT TRAINING?
A: AR 350-30.

25. Q: HOW MANY ARTICLES ARE THERE IN THE CODE OF CONDUCT?
A: Six.

26. Q: WHAT IS ESSENTIAL TO DISCIPLINE IN A PRISONER OF WAR CAMP?
A: Strong leadership.

Enlisted Promotion

1. Q: WHAT ARE THE OBJECTIVES OF THE ARMY PROMOTION SYSTEM?
1) Fill authorized enlisted spaces with qualified soldiers.
2) Provide for career progression and rank which is in line with potential.
3) Recognize the best qualified soldier which will attract and retain the highest caliber soldier for a career in the Army.
4) Preclude promoting the soldier who is not productive or not best qualified.
5) Provide an equitable system for all soldiers.

2. Q: WHO HAS THE AUTHORITY TO ADVANCE OR PROMOTE ASSIGNED SOLDIERS TO GRADES E-2 THROUGH E-4?
A: Unit Commander.

3. Q: WHO HAS THE AUTHORITY TO PROMOTE TO GRADES E-5 AND E-6?
A: Field grade commanders of any unit authorized a commander in grade of Lieutenant Colonel (O5) or higher.

4. Q: WHAT STATEMENT MUST BE INCLUDED IN ALL PROMOTION ORDERS TO GRADES E-4 THROUGH E-6?
A: Promotion is not valid and will be revoked if the soldier is not promotable on the effective date of promotion.

5. Q: CAN A PERSON BE DENIED PROMOTION IF THEY FAIL TO TAKE AN SQT TEST DUE TO THEIR OWN FAULT?

A: Yes, the promotion authority will determine if it is their fault.

6. Q: **WHAT DATE IS USED TO COMPUTE TIME-IN-SERVICE FOR ACTIVE DUTY PERSONNEL?**
A: Basic Active Service Date (BASD); however, this is immaterial since time in service is no longer computed for promotion points.

7. Q: **HOW LONG DOES A SOLDIER HAVE TO SERVE ON ACTIVE DUTY BEFORE HE/SHE CAN BE ADVANCED TO E-2?**
A: Six months of active federal service.

8. Q: **WHAT IS THE NORMAL TIME IN GRADE AND TIME IN SERVICE REQUIREMENTS FOR ADVANCEMENT TO PRIVATE FIRST CLASS E-3?**
A: 12 months time in service and 4 months time in grade.

9. Q: **ARE SQT SCORES NEEDED TO PROMOTE TO SPECIALIST FOUR (E-4)?**
A: No.

10. Q: **WHO ANNOUNCES LIMITATIONS FOR PROMOTION TO SPECIALIST FOUR(E-4)?**
A: HQ Department of the Army.

11. Q: **IF A SOLDIER RECEIVES 59 OR LESS ON HIS FIRST SQT TEST, WILL HE BE REMOVED FROM THE LOCAL RECOMMENDED PROMOTION LIST?**
A: No, Promotion points will be adjusted at the next recomputation.

12. Q: **ARE LOCAL POSITION VACANCIES REQUIRED FOR PROMOTION TO THE NEXT HIGHER GRADE?**
A: No.

13. Q: **WHAT FORM WOULD YOU USE TO RECOMMEND A PERSON FOR PROMOTION?**
A: DA form 4187 (Personnel Action) or DA Form 2496 (Disposition Form).

14. Q: **WHAT THREE THINGS MUST A RECOMMENDING OFFICIAL INDICATE ON HIS RECOMMENDATION?**
A: 1) The soldiers recommended meets the promotion criteria of Chapter 7, AR 600-200.
2) He understands the soldier may be reassigned or change duty position.
3) He is willing to release the soldier to promotion.

15. Q: **WHO APPROVES OR DISAPPROVES PROMOTION RECOMMENDATIONS?**
A: The promotion authority.

16. Q: IF A PROMOTION RECOMMENDATION INCLUDING WAIVER IS DISAPPROVED, IT WILL BE RETURNED THROUGH CHANNELS TO THE RECOMMENDING OFFICIAL WITH REASONS FOR DISAPPROVAL STATED CLEARLY AND CONCISELY. WHAT MUST THE RECOMMENDING OFFICIAL THEN DO?
A: The recommending official will advise the soldier of the reasons for disapproval, point out deficiencies and suggest ways for improving performance. After this, a statement will be prepared and the soldier will sign it affirming that he has been counseled on his promotion status and deficiencies.

17. Q: WHEN IS A PROMOTION POINT WORKSHEET (DA FORM 3355) PREPARED?
A: When promotion recommendations and waivers are approved.

18. Q: HOW OFTEN ARE PROMOTION BOARDS CONVENED?
A: Monthly, except when no soldier is recommended for board action.

19. Q: A PROMOTION BOARD MUST CONSIST OF AT LEAST HOW MANY MEMBERS?
A: At least three voting members and a recorder without a vote.

20. Q: WHO WILL BE THE PRESIDENT OF A MIXED PROMOTION BOARD?
A: The senior member, preferably a field grade officer.

21. Q: THE SENIOR MEMBER OF AN ALL ENLISTED PROMOTION BOARD MUST BE WHAT GRADE?
A: Command Sergeant Major.

22. Q: HOW SOON AFTER SELECTION ARE PERSONNEL ELIGIBLE FOR PROMOTION TO E5 AND E6?
A: Soldiers will be eligible for promotion on the first day of the third month following selection.

23. Q: HOW OFTEN WILL A SOLDIER WITH VALID RECOMMENDATION LIST STATUS FOR PROMOTION TO GRADES E5 AND E6 BE RECOMPUTED?
A: Promotion points will be recomputed twice yearly without local promotion board action.

24. Q: HOW SOON AFTER A SOLDIER APPEARS ON A CURRENT RECOMMENDED LIST FOR PROMOTION CAN HE/SHE REQUEST REEVALUATION?
A: Three months or more after the soldier appears on a current recommended list.

25. Q: IF A SOLDIER IS ON THE RECOMMENDED LIST FOR PROMOTION TO E5 OR E6 AND MEETS THE PROMOTION POINT CUT OFF SCORE, WHO WILL PROMOTE THE INDIVIDUAL IF HE/SHE IS IN TRANSIT?
A: The individual will be promoted by the gaining promotion authority.

26. Q: WHAT IS THE SERVICE REMAINING OBLIGATION FOR PROMOTION TO GRADES E5 AND E6?
A: For promotion to E5, 3 months; for promotion to E6, 12 months.

27. Q: WHAT ARE THE SECURITY REQUIREMENTS FOR PROMOTION TO GRADE E7?
A: The soldier must have a security clearance required by the MOS in which to be promoted.

28. Q: WHAT ARE THE SECURITY CLEARANCE REQUIREMENTS FOR PROMOTION TO GRADES E8 OR E9?
A: The soldier must have a favorable National Agency Check (NAC) completed or have a final SECRET security clearance or higher.

29. Q: HQDA ANNOUNCES THE RESULTS OF SELECTION BOARDS BY A COMMAND LETTER. WHAT INCLOSURE WILL THIS LETTER CONTAIN?
A: 1) Letter of instruction.
   2) Board membership.
   3) Recommended list.

30. Q: DO SOLDIERS PROMOTED TO GRADES E7, E8, AND E9 INCUR A SERVICE OBLIGATION? IF SO, HOW LONG?
A: Yes, soldiers incur a two year service obligation.

31. Q: WHO MAY APPOINT QUALIFIED SOLDIERS AS ACTING CORPORALS, E4 AND SERGEANTS E5?
A: Company, troop, battery and separate detachment commanders.

32. Q: WHO CAN APPOINT AN ACTING CORPORAL, E4 OR SERGEANT E5?
A: Company, troop, battery and separate detachment commanders.

33. Q: IS THERE A GRADE RESTRICTION FOR APPOINTMENT AS AN ACTING CORPORAL, E4 OR SERGEANT E5?
A: Yes, the soldier may not be more than one grade lower than the one to which appointed.

Reenlistment

1. Q: WHAT REGULATION IS USED IN DETERMINING ELIGIBILITY FOR REENLISTMENT?
A: AR 601-280.

2. Q: WHO DETERMINES THE QUALIFICATION FOR REENLISTMENT IN THE REGULAR ARMY?
A: Secretary of the Army.

3. Q: WHEN SHOULD REENLISTMENT ORIENTATION BEGIN?
A: On the day the individual reports to the unit.

4. Q: WHAT FORM IS USED TO RECORD REENLISTMENT INTERVIEWS?
A: DA Form 1315.

5. Q: IF A SOLDIER IS ELIGIBLE/INELIGIBLE FOR REENLISTMENT, BUT NOT RECOMMENDED, THE COMMANDER MUST DO WHAT?
A: Promptly initiate a bar to reenlistment.

6. Q: A BAR TO REENLIST NORMALLY SHOULD NOT BE INITIATED AGAINST AN INDIVIDUAL WHO HAS BEEN ASSIGNED TO A UNIT LESS THAN HOW MANY DAYS?
A: 90.

7. Q: NORMALLY A BAR WILL NOT BE INITIATED WITHIN HOW MANY DAYS OF PCS OR ETS?
A: 30.

8. Q: WHAT FORM IS USED TO PREPARE A BAR TO REENLIST?
A: DA Form 4126R.

9. Q: WHO MAY INITIATE A BAR?
A: Any commander in the chain of command.

10. Q: WHEN A BAR TO REENLIST IS INITIATED THE INDIVIDUAL CONCERNED HAS HOW MANY DAYS TO PREPARE A STATEMENT AND COLLECTION OF DOCUMENTS TO BE SUBMITTED IN HIS OWN BEHALF?
A: 15 Days.

11. Q: WHEN A BAR TO REENLISTMENT HAS BEEN APPROVED THE INDIVIDUAL HAS HOW MANY DAYS TO APPEAL?

A: 15 Days.

12. Q: WHO MAY APPROVE A BAR FOR A SOLDIER WITH LESS THAN 10 YEARS SERVICE OF ETS?
A: 1st commander, O5 or above, in SM normal chain of command or commander exercising SCMA which ever is in the most direct line to the soldier.

13. Q: MAY A SOLDIER WITH A BAR TO REENLIST BE EXTENDED?
A: Yes.

14. Q: WHEN A BAR TO REENLIST IS APPROVED, THE CUSTODIAN OF THE INDIVIDUALS RECORD WILL PLACE A SIGNED COPY OF THE CERTIFICATE IN THE INDIVIDUAL'S MPRJ AND MAKE AN ENTRY ON THE DA FORM 2-1 THAT SAYS?
A: "Not recommended for further service."

15. Q: WHO HAS THE AUTHORITY TO VOID A BAR TO REENLIST?
A: The same authority that approved the certificate.

16. Q: AFTER A BAR TO REENLIST HAS BEEN APPROVED AND THE INITIAL REVIEWS HAVE BEEN COMPLETED THE COMMANDER MUST SUBSEQUENTLY REVIEW THE BAR TO REENLIST, HOW OFTEN?
A: Every 6 months.

17. Q: WHEN MAY A RECOMMENDATION TO VOID A BAR TO REENLIST BE SUBMITTED?
A: At any time by the individuals unit commander, if he feels the individual is worthy of retention.

18. Q: WHEN MUST THE COMMANDER INITIALLY REVIEW A BAR TO REENLIST?
A: 6 months after approval or 30 days prior to individuals PCS or ETS which ever occurs first.

19. Q: WHAT MUST THE COMMANDER DO AFTER COMPLETION OF A REVIEW TO A BAR TO REENLIST?
A: The commander must inform the individual concerned that the bar has been reviewed and what action was taken.

20. Q: WHEN AN INDIVIDUAL IS SEPARATED FROM THE ARMY WITH A BAR TO REENLIST, IN EFFECT THE DD FORM 214 WILL BE CODED WITH WHAT REENLISTMENT CODE?
A: RE3 unless separated with more than 18 years service then the code will be RE4.

21. Q: WHO MUST APPROVE A REQUEST FOR REENLISTMENT?
A: The individual's immediate commander.

22. Q: WHAT FORM IS USED TO REQUEST REENLISTMENT?
A: DA Form 3340.

23. Q: WHAT FORM IS USED TO REQUEST EXTENSION OF ENLISTMENT?
A: DA Form 3340.

24. Q: WHAT ARE THE SEVEN BASIC ELIGIBILITY REQUIREMENTS FOR REENLISTMENT?
A: Age, citizenship, trainability requirements, education, medical, waivable/non waivable administrative disqualification, grade.

25. Q: WHAT ARE THE EDUCATION REQUIREMENTS FOR REENLISTMENT?
A: Applicant must meet education requirements for the specific option for which reenlisted.

26. Q: WHAT IS THE MAX NUMBER OF DAYS AN INDIVIDUAL ETS CAN EXCEED THE RETENTION INELIGIBILITY POINT FOR GRADE WITHOUT AN APPROVED WAIVER?
A: 29 days.

27. Q: WHO MUST TAKE AN SQT TEST IN ORDER TO REENLIST?
A: Soldiers for whom there is an SQT available in their PMOS/skill level, and who are eligible for SQT testing in accordance with CH5, AR 600-200.

28. Q: WHAT ARE THE AUTHORIZED REENLISTMENT PERIODS?
A: 3, 4, 5, or 6 years.

29. Q: WHO NORMALLY SELECTS THE NUMBER OF YEARS AN INDIVIDUAL WILL REENLIST FOR?
A: The applicant.

30. Q: WHO MAY ADMINISTER THE OATH OF ENLISTMENT?
A: A commissioned officer.

31. Q: MAY A REENLISTMENT BE SENSATIONALIZED TO PUBLICIZE THE EVENT (i.e. parachuting, climbing utility poles, etc)?
A: No, reenlistment will be made an official ceremony.

32. Q: WHO CHOOSES THE OFFICER ADMINISTERING THE OATH OF ENLISTMENT?
A: The reenlistee.

33. Q: WHAT REQUIREMENTS MUST A SOLDIER NORMALLY MEET IN ORDER TO EXTEND?

A: Must be otherwise qualified for reenlistment in accordance with CH2 AR 601-280.

34. Q: HOW LONG MAY A SOLDIER BE EXTENDED?
A: Extension will be limited to the minimum time required to achieve the desired purpose.

35. Q: HOW LONG MAY A SOLDIER BE EXTENDED FOR "BEST INTEREST OF THE SERVICE" OF ANY ONE ENLISTMENT PERIOD?
A: 12 months.

36. Q: WHO IS NOT REQUIRED TO SIGN A COUNSELING STATEMENT REFUSING TO TAKE ACTION TO MEET LENGTH OF SERVICE REQUIREMENTS?
A: Initial termers.

37. Q: MUST AN INDIVIDUAL, WHO REFUSES TO TAKE ACTION TO COMPLY WITH ORDERS, SIGN THE COUNSELING STATEMENT?
A: No, if SM refuses to sign the acknowledgement, this will be indicated on the statement and signed by the person witnessing the refusal.

38. Q: WHAT EFFECT DOES REFUSAL TO TAKE ACTION TO COMPLY WITH ORDER HAVE ON THE SOLDIER?
A: 1) SM is placed in a nonpromotable status.
2) Prohibits SM from enlisting for at least 93 days after discharge.
3) Results in an RE code 3A which requires waiver by Department of the Army.
4) Prohibits extension.
5) Prohibits SM from applying for commissioned or warrant officer program.

39. Q: MAY A SOLDIER WAIVE HIS REENLISTMENT COMMITMENTS?
A: Yes.

40. Q: WHEN A SOLDIER WIVES HIS REENLISTMENT COMMITMENTS, HE IS THEN SUBJECT TO WHAT?
A: The needs of the service.

41. Q: WHEN MAY A SOLDIER, SERVING ON HIS FIRST TERM OF ACTIVE FEDERAL SERVICE, REENLIST?
A: During the last 6 months of current term of service.

42. Q: WHEN A SOLDIER IN CONUS REENLISTS FOR PRESENT DUTY ASSIGNMENT, IS HE GUARANTEED A ONE YEAR STABILIZATION?
A: No, initial assignment only.

**43. Q: WHEN A SOLDIER REENLISTS FOR AN OVERSEAS AREA OF CHOICE, IS HE GUARANTEED A SPECIFIC UNIT/DETACHMENT IN HIS

AREA OF CHOICE?
A: No.

44. Q: WHAT REENLISTMENT AUTHORITY IS USED TO GUARANTEE A ONE-YEAR STABILIZATION FOR A SOLDIER REENLISTING WITHIN CONUS?
A: CONUS Station of choice reenlistment option.

45. Q: WHO IS ELIGIBLE TO REENLIST FOR THE UNITED STATES ARMY CONUS TO CONUS STATION OF CHOICE REENLISTMENT OPTION?
A: Soldiers serving on their initial enlistment only.

46. Q: WHAT FORM IS PREPARED FOR PERSONS EXTENDING IN THE REGULAR ARMY?
A: DA Form 1695 (oath of extension of enlistment).

47. Q: WHAT FORMS ARE PREPARED FOR MEMBERS WHO IMMEDIATELY REENLIST?
A: DD Form 4 series.

48. Q: WHO IS CONSIDERED AN INITIAL TERMER?
A: Individuals serving on an initial term of Active Federal Military Service.

49. Q: WHO IS CONSIDERED A MID-TERM CAREERIST?
A: Individuals serving on a 2nd or subsequent enlistment with 10 or less years of service at ETS.

NONCOMMISSIONED OFFICER REORTING SYSTEM

1. Q: TRUE OR FALSE: DA CIRCULAR 623-88-1 COVERS THE NONCOMMISSIONED OFFICER EVALUATION REPORTING SYSTEM?
A: True (Located in the Personnel Evaluations Update).

2. Q: WHAT IS THE TITLE OF DA FORM 2166-7?
A: The Noncommissioned Officer Evaluation Report, known as the NCO-ER.

3. Q: WHAT ARE SOME REASONS FOR THE NEW NCO-ER SYSTEM?
A: 1) Ensures the best selection of NCOs to serve in positions of

responsibility. 2) It provides formal recognition for performance of duty. 3) Provides information for school selections, promotions, assignments, and qualitative management.

4. Q: HOW SHOULD A RATING SCHEME BE PUBLISHED?
A: By name or duty position.

5. Q: WHERE IS THE RATING SCHEME POSTED?
A: In the unit.

6. Q: WHEN IS AN NCO-ER SUBMITTED IN TIME TO REACH FT. BENJAMIN HARRISON?
A: No later than 60 days after the ending month of the report.

7. Q: THE MINIMUM AUTHORIZED PERIOD FOR AN EER IS 3 RATED MONTHS. WHAT TWO REPORTS REQUIRE ONLY 30 DAYS?
A: 1) Special.
   2) Relief for cause.

8. Q: WHAT IS A RATING SCHEME? A: A rating scheme is the chain of evaluators that rates the NCO. Rating schemes must correspond as nearly as possible to the chain of command and supervision within an organization.

9. Q: TRUE OR FALSE: COMMANDERS WILL ENSURE THAT ALL OFFICIAL RATING SCHEMES ARE PUBLISHED BY NAME SO THAT ALL NCOs KNOW THEIR RATER.
A: True (DA CIR 623-88-1).

10. Q: THERE ARE TIMES WHEN AN NCO/RATER WILL NOT BE RATED AND WILL NOT BE ALLOWED TO RATE OTHER NCOs. WHEN IS THIS TRUE? A: When the person is:

   1) AWOL

   2) Break in active duty of 12 months or less

   3) Confinement

   4) In transit between duty stations

   5) Missing in Action

   6) TDY or Special Duty

11. Q: WHEN IS AN ANNUAL REPORT REQUIRED?
A: Twelve months after the ending month of the last report.

12. Q: WHAT THREE SITUATIONS REQUIRED A CHANGE OF RATER IF THE 3 MONTH MINIMUM RATING PERIOD REQUIREMENTS ARE MET?
A: 1) Change of designated rater.
   2) Extended TDY or SD (3 months or more).
   3) ETS.

13. Q: TRUE OR FALSE: EVALUATIONS WILL BE GIVEN TO NCOs FOR PERIODS WHEN THEY WERE A PRISONER OF WAR.
A: False.

14. Q: IF AN NCO VOLUNTARILY ENTERS THE ALCOHOL AND DRUG ABUSE PREVENTION AND CONTROL PROGRAM SHOULD THE SOLDIER BE PENALIZED BY MENTION OF THE ADAPCD IN THE NCO-ER?
A: No, by doing so could discourage voluntary entry in the ADAPCP.

15. Q: WHEN WILL AN INITIAL, ANNUAL, OR COMPLETE RECORD BE SIGNED BY THE RATER?
A: Not prior to the 1st day of the month following the closing month.

16. Q: IS IT POSSIBLE THAT AN NCO-ER CAN OBTAIN CLASSIFIED INFORMATION.
A: Yes, but not normally. If so, these cases will contain downgrading instructions and each section will be marked to show the level of classification.

17. Q: WHEN WILL A COMPLETE-THE-RECORD REPORT BE SUBMITTED?
A: At the option of the rater a report may be submitted on a soldier who is about to be considered by a DA selection board, school or CSM selection.

18. Q: WHAT ARE THE THREE REQUIREMENTS NEEDED TO SUBMIT A COMPLETE-THE-RECORD REPORT?
   1) Must be in the zone of consideration (primary or secondary) for a DA centralized promotion board, zone of consideration for a school or CSM selection board.
   2) In current duty position and under the same rater for at least 6 months.
   3) Not have previously received a report for his or her current duty assignment.

19. Q: NAME TWO QUALIFICATIONS NEEDED TO BE RATER?
A: 1) First line supervisor of the rater soldier for a minimum period of 3 months.
   2) In pay grade E5 or higher, if military and senior to the rated soldier by either pay grade or grade in rank.

20. Q: IF AN NCO FEELS AS THOUGH HE/SHE WAS GIVEN AN NCO-ER THAT WAS NOT FAIR, WHAT IS THE PROCEDURE THE NCO SHOULD TAKE? A: Appeal.

21. Q: WHAT GRADE MUST A CIVILIAN RATER BE?
A: GS-6 and above.

22. Q: ARE MEMBERS OF ALLIED FORCES AUTHORIZED TO BE RATERS?
A: No.

23. Q: NAME TWO QUALIFICATIONS NEEDED TO BE AN ENDORSER.
A: 1) In direct line of supervision of the rated soldier for a minimum period of three months.
   2) Senior to the rater in grade or date of rank.

24. Q: WHEN IS AN ENDORSER NOT REQUIRED?
A: When the rater is a general officer, officer of flag rank, or U.S. civilian with Senior Service (SES) rank and precedence.

25. Q: WHAT ARE THE QUALIFICATIONS NEEDED TO BE A REVIEWER?
A: 1) A commissioned officer, warrant officer, command sergeant major in the direct line of supervision and senior in grade or date of rank to both the rater and endorser.
   2) Field grade officer for special reports.
   3) Civilian if either rater or endorser is a uniformed army official.

26. Q: WHAT IF THE RATHER OR ENDORSER IS A GENERAL OFFICER, WHO REVIEWS THE REPORT?
A: He will also act as reviewer and complete Part V D of the report.

27. Q: TRUE OR FALSE: THE APPEALS SYSTEM PROTECTS THE ARMY'S INTEREST AND ENSURES FAIRNESS TO THE NCO. AT THE SAME TIME, IT AVOIDS IMPUGNING THE INTEGRITY OR JUDGEMENT OF THE RATING OFFICIALS.
A: True.

28. Q: IF AN NCO HAS ANY QUESTIONS PERTAINING TO THE NCO-ER, WHERE CAN HE/SHE OBTAIN INFORMATION? A:
1) DA CIR 623-88-1 (Personnel Evaluations Update)
   2) Chain of Command
   3) Army Learning Center

29. Q: CAN AN NCO-ER BE HAND CARRIED BY THE RATED SOLDIER TO

THE GAINING MILPO OR RC COMMAND FOR COMPLETION?
A: In no case.

30. Q: DOES THE SOLDIER RECEIVE A COPY OF HIS/HER NCO EVALUATION REPORT?
A: Yes, it may be given to him/her personally or forwarded to him/her in a sealed envelope or mailed (1st class).

31. Q: DOES A COPY OF THE NCO-ER GO INTO THE 201 FILE?
A: Yes, and will be filed in the permanent section of the soldiers Military Personnel Records Jacket (MPRJ).

33. Q: MAY A COMMANDER APPOINT A U.S. CIVILIAN AS A RATER WHEN THE SOLDIER DOES NOT HAVE A FIRST-LINE MILITARY SUPERVISOR?
A: Yes, as long as the U.S. civilian is GS-6 or above, and the civilian is in the best position to accurately evaluate the NCO's performance.

34. Q: WHO NORMALLY ORIGINATES AN APPEAL OF AN EER?
A: The rated soldier.

35. Q: CAN ACTIVE ARMY APPEALS BE SUBMITTED ELSEWHERE?
A: Yes, if appeals do not meet time restrictions they may be submitted to the Army Board for correction of military records.

36. Q: CAN SM REQUEST ASSISTANCE IF DESIRED?
A: Yes, from MILPO or unit commander.

37. Q: HOW WILL THE ADMINISTRATIVE AND NARRATIVE PORTIONS OF THE NCO-ER BE PREPARED?
A: By typing or machine printing.

38. Q: ARE FACSIMILE SIGNATURES AUTHORIZED?
A: No, they are not authorized.

39. Q: ARE AWARDS OR LETTERS OF COMMENDATION, APPRECIATION, MEDICAL DOCUMENTS, ETC. AUTHORIZED AS INCLOSURES TO AN EER?
A: No, they are not authorized.

40. Q: HOW WILL AN INCLOSURE BE PREPARED?
A: 8 1/2 by 11 inch bond paper and will include the following:
    1) Rated soldier's full name, SSN, and grade.
    2) The period of report.
    3) Authentication by the originator.

41. Q: WHEN WILL NCO-ER'S NOT NORMALLY BE PREPARED FOR INDIVIDUALS?
A: 1) Within 6 months of an approved voluntary retirement date.
    2) Have requested retirement in lieu of accepting PCS assignment or reassignment.

42. Q: WHAT ARE THREE REASONS FOR NON-RATED PERIODS?
A: 1) AWOL/desertion.
    2) In transit between duty stations, including leave, travel and temporary duty.
    3) Lack of rater qualifications.

43. Q: IF THE SOLDIER SERVES AS A MEMBER AT A COURT-MARTIAL WILL IT BE REFERENCED ON HIS EER?
A: No, that is not authorized.

Alcohol and Drug Abuse Prevention and Control Program

1. Q: A COMMANDER MAY SUSPEND A PCS MOVEMENT OF AN ARMY SERVICE MEMBER FOR UP TO 30 DAYS TO OBTAIN NECESSARY REHABILITATION.
A: True.

2. Q: NAME TWO OF THE THREE OBJECTIVES FOR LAW ENFORCEMENT AND DRUG SUPPRESSION.
A: 1) Eliminate the supply of illegal drugs.
    2) Identify and apprehend individuals who illegally posses, use, or traffic the drugs.
    3) Prevent alcohol and other drug related crimes, incidents and traffic accidents.

3. Q: IF A SERVICE MEMBER WHO INITIALLY SEEKS HELP FROM AN ACTIVITY OR INDIVIDUAL OTHER THAN HIS OR HER UNIT COMMANDER, MUST THAT INDIVIDUAL NOTIFY THE SERVICE MEMBERS UNIT COM-

MANDER AND INSTALLATION ADCO? YES OR NO?
A: Yes, immediately.

4. Q: A MEDICAL EVALUATION TO DETERMINE THE EXTENT OF ALCOHOL OR OTHER DRUG ABUSE MAY BE REQUESTED ONLY BY THE COMMANDER. TRUE OR FALSE?
A: False, the commander, clinical director, counselor, or the service member may request a medical evaluation by a physician at any time.

5. Q: WHAT IS COMMAND IDENTIFICATION?
A: This is where a commander observes, suspects, or otherwise becomes aware of an individual whose job performance, social conduct, interpersonal relations, physical fitness, or health appears to be adversely affected because of alcohol or other drugs.

6. Q: IS REHABILITATION OF ALCOHOL AND OTHER DRUG ABUSE A COMMAND RESPONSIBILITY? YES OR NO?
A: Yes.

7. Q: WHEN DOES REHABILITATION BEGIN?
A: Rehabilitation begins when an individual is identified as being involved with alcohol and other drug abuse or illegal use.

8. Q: COUNSELING WILL BE SCHEDULED AT CLIENT'S CONVENIENCE. TRUE OR FALSE?
A: False, appointments will not interfere with clients job or duty requirements.

9. Q: WHERE CAN A SERVICE MEMBER WHILE ON LEAVE, TDY, OR PCS STATUS WHO REQUIRES DETOXIFICATION SEEK HELP OR MEDICAL ATTENTION?
A: Service member will be admitted to the nearest military medical treatment facility. (Upon completion of detoxification, the service member will be returned to his or her unit for rehabilitation).

10. Q: WHAT IS THE DEFINITION OF EXEMPTION?
A: Exemption is an immunity from disciplinary action under the UCMJ or from administration type separation with less than an honorable discharge as a result of certain occurrences of alcohol abuse or drug misuse or possession of drugs incidental to personal use.

11. Q: NAME THE AR WHICH GOVERNS THE ALCOHOL AND DRUG ABUSE PREVENTION AND CONTROL PROGRAM. (ADAPCP)
A: AR 600-85.

12. Q: WHAT IS DRUG ABUSE?
A: The illegal, wrongful, or improper use of any narcotic substance or its derivative, cannabis or its derivative, other controlled substance or dangerous

drugs. This includes the improper use of drugs prescribed by a physician.

13. Q: WHAT IS DRUG DEPENDENCE?
A: The need for a drug which results from the continuous or periodic use of the drug.

14. Q: IN THE ADAPCP PROGRAM, WHAT IS CONFIDENTIAL INFORMATION?
A: Personal information revealed by a client to a counselor which will be used only for counseling or official ADAPCP purposes in accordance with Federal regulations.

15. Q: WHAT IS A MEDICAL EVALUATION?
A: An examination of an individual by a physician to determine whether there is evidence of alcohol or other drug abuse or dependency.

16. Q: WHAT IS A COMMUNITY COUNSELING CENTER?
A: The facility where local ADAPCP counseling services are provided.

17. Q: WHAT IS COMMAND CONSULTATION?
A: The process through which members of the ADAPCP staff and/or the MEDCEN/MEDDAC staff meet with an immediate commander to discuss/or recommend a course of action concerning a service member.

18. Q: WHAT IS MEDICAL IDENTIFICATION?
A: Apparent alcohol or other drug abuse noted by a physician during routine or emergency medical treatment.

19. Q: WHAT IS AWARENESS EDUCATION?
A: Education which aims at increasing knowledge of the effects and consequences of alcohol or other drugs on both an organizational and personal level.

20. Q: WHAT IS A CLINICAL CONSULTANT?
A: The military physician who is responsible for providing, coordinating and supervising consultative and medical support to the ADAPCP for the MEDCEN/MEDDAC Commander.

21. Q: WHAT IS ALCOHOL ABUSE?
A: Any irresponsible use of an alcoholic beverage which leads to misconduct, unacceptable social behavior, or impairment of individual's performance of duty, physical or mental health, financial responsibility, or personal relationships.

22. Q: WHAT IS ALCOHOLISM?
A: Treatment or treatable, progressive condition or illness, characterized by excessive consumption of alcohol to the extent that the individual's physical and mental health, personal relationships, social conduct, or job performance

are impaired.

23. Q: WHAT IS THE ALCOHOL AND DRUG CONTROL OFFICER (ADCO)?
A: The person having staff responsibilities for implementing, operating, and monitoring the ADAPCP at MACOM, installation, or major tenant unit levels.

24. Q: WHAT IS THE JOB OF THE EDUCATION COORDINATOR (EDCO)?
A: The individual who is responsible to the ADCO for administering an alcohol and other drug abuse prevention education and training programs.

25. Q: IN THE ADAPCP PROGRAM, WHAT DOES THE WORD ENROLLMENT MEAN?
A: The formal action taken by a commander to enter a service member into the ADAPCP.

26. Q: WHAT IS THE REHABILITATION TEAM?
A: An informal coordinating group consisting of the client's unit commander or his designee, immediate supervisor, and counselor plus other appropriate personnel as required (i.e., clinical director, chaplain, physician).

27. Q: ADAPCP RECORDS ARE MEDICAL RECORDS AND ARE PROTECTED BY AR 40-66. ALL ADAPCP RECORDS WILL BE MAINTAINED AND STORED FOR A PERIOD OF 6 MONTHS AFTER CLOSING THE CASE BY ADAPCP PER AR 340-18-9. TRUE OR FALSE?
A: False, records will be maintained 12 months after case is closed by ADAPCP.

28. Q: COMMANDER SEEKING INFORMATION FROM AN INDIVIDUAL'S ADAPCP RECORDS MUST SPECIFY THEIR NEED TO KNOW SPECIFIC INFORMATION. WHO MUST THEIR REQUEST BE SUBMITTED TO?
A: Their request must be made to the responsible MEDCEN/MEDDAC commander for proper release of information.

29. Q: WHAT GOVERNS THE ALCOHOL AND OTHER DRUG ABUSE BY AVIATION PERSONNEL, AND ALSO IS OF SPECIAL CONCERN BECAUSE OF ITS IMPACT ON AVIATION SAFETY?
A: AR 40-501, established medical fitness standards for aviation personnel.

30. Q: CAN AN INDIVIDUAL REENLIST WHILE ENROLLED IN THE ADAPCP PROGRAM?
A: Yes, a waiver is required to reenlist in the Army.

31. Q: COULD AN ENLISTED MEMBER BECOME A ADAPCP COUNSELOR?
A: Yes.

32. Q: WHAT RANK IS QUALIFIED TO BE A COUNSELOR?
A: E-5 and above and MOS qualified.

33. Q: CAN A RECOVERING ALCOHOLIC OR DRUG ABUSER BE SELECTED AS A COUNSELOR?
A: Yes, if they are alcohol or drug free for a minimum of 2 years.

34. Q: CAN A COMMANDER REQUEST ALCOHOL AND OTHER DRUG AWARENESS EDUCATION FOR PERSONNEL SUSPECTED OF INVOLVEMENT WITH DRUGS OR OF ABUSING ALCOHOL?
A: Yes, a commander may request drug and alcohol education even without a specific incident upon which to base the referral.

35. Q: THE THREE LAW ENFORCEMENT OBJECTIVES FOR DRUG SUPPRESSION ARE:
  1) **Eliminate the supply of illegal drugs.**
  2) **Identify and apprehend individuals who illegally possess, use of, or traffic in drugs.**
  3) **Prevent alcohol and other drug-related crimes, incidents, and traffic accidents.**
     TRUE OR FALSE?
A: True.

36. Q: ARE THE M.P.'S, CID, SPECIAL AGENTS OR ANY OTHER INVESTIGATIVE PERSONNEL ALLOWED TO SOLICIT INFORMATION FROM CLIENTS IN THE ADAPCP PROGRAM?
A: No, unless they volunteer to provide information and assistance.

37. Q: CHAPTER I, TITLE 42, CODE OF FEDERAL REGULATIONS, PROHIBITS UNDERCOVER AGENTS FROM ENROLLING IN OR OTHERWISE INFILTRATING AN ALCOHOL OR OTHER DRUG TREATMENT OR REHABILITATION PROGRAM FOR THE PURPOSE OF LAW ENFORCEMENT ACTIVITIES. TRUE OF FALSE?
A: True.

38. Q: FOR REHABILITATION PURPOSES, CAN A M.P., CID, OR OTHER INVESTIGATIVE PERSONNEL WHO HAS AN ACTUAL ALCOHOL OR OTHER DRUG RELATED PROBLEM ENROLL IN THE ADAPCP PROGRAM?
A: Yes, their law enforcement status must be made known to the ADCO at the time of their enrollment.

39. Q: WHAT IS A CPC?
A: Civilian Program Coordinator.

40. Q: WHAT IS A CPA?
A: Civilian Program Administrator.

41. Q: WHAT IS AN EDCO?
A: Educational Coordinator.

42. Q: WHAT IS THE USACIDC?
A: United States Army Criminal Investigator Command.

43. Q: THE USE OF CANNABIS BY IN SERVICE PERSONNEL IS NOT A VIOLATION OF THE UNIFORM CODE OF MILITARY JUSTICE (UCMJ). TRUE OR FALSE?
A: False, it is a violation of the UCMJ.

44. Q: WHAT IS USADATT?
A United States Army Alcohol and Drug Abuse Team Training.

45. Q: WHAT IS CMHA?
A: Community Mental Health Activities.

46. Q: A MILITARY PERSONS RIGHTS ARE DESCRIBED UNDER ARTICLE 31 UCMJ. TRUE OR FALSE?
A: True.

47. Q: WHEN WAS THE DOD BIOCHEMICAL TESTING PROGRAM ESTABLISHED AND BY WHOM?
A: In 1971 by the Secretary of Defense.

48. Q: BIOCHEMICAL TESTING OF URINE CAN DETECT VARIOUS DRUGS. NAME THREE.
A: 1) Amphetamines.
   2) Barbiturates.
   3) Opiates.
   4) Methaqualone.
   5) Phencyclinine.
   6) Cocaine.

49. Q: THERE ARE THREE ENROLLMENT PROGRAMS, TRACK I, II, III. WHAT IS THE LENGTH OF TIME FOR EACH TRACK?
A: Track I will not exceed 30 days, Track II- minimum of 30 days, Track III is for 360 days.

50. Q: WHAT IS ECSP AND WHAT DOES IT DO?
A: Employee Counseling Services Program can encourage early identification and referral of alcohol and drug abuse problems and eliminate the need for supervisor's to determine the nature of an employee's problem before making a referral.

Nuclear, Biological and Chemical Warfare

1. Q: WHAT IS THE BEST PROTECTION AGAINST BIOLOGICAL WARFARE?
A: Immunization and personal hygiene. Troop indoctrination.

2. Q: THERE ARE SEVERAL TYPES OF TERRAIN AND WEATHER CONDITIONS WHICH FAVOR GAS ATTACKS. WHAT ARE THEY?
A: Low ground containing heavy vegetation.
   Foggy weather.
   Foggy weather with approaching or parallel winds from 3 to 12 miles per hour.

3. Q: WHEN AN ATOMIC BOMB EXPLODES WHAT THREE THINGS CAUSE DAMAGE?
A: Heat- Thermal radiation (heat and light)
   Blast
   Radiation- Nuclear radiation

4. Q: ARE THERE ANY SELF AID MEASURES YOU CAN USE FOR RADIATION SICKNESS?
A: No.

5. Q: WHAT ARE THE SYMPTOMS OF NERVE GAS CONTAMINATION?
A: Excessive sweating.
   The pupils of the eyes shrinking to pinpoints.
   Tightness in the chest and difficulty in breathing.
   Runny nose.

6. Q: WHAT IS THE SHAPE OF ALL CONTAMINATION MARKERS?
A: Triangular.

7. Q: NAME THE VARIOUS TYPES OF NUCLEAR BURSTS.
A: Air burst.
   Surface burst.
   Subsurface burst.

8. Q: ALL NBC MARKERS ARE OF THE SAME SHAPE AND SIZE. DEFINE THEIR SIZE.
A: An isosceles triangle with the point facing downward, 8 inches X 11 1/2 inches X 8 inches.

9. Q: NBC MARKERS FACE IN WHAT DIRECTION?
A: Away from the danger zone.

10. Q: WHAT PROTECTIVE MEASURES SHOULD AN INDIVIDUAL TAKE UPON NOTICING A NUCLEAR BLAST WHILE IN AN OPEN AREA?
A: Lay down and cover all exposed parts of the body.

11. Q: WHAT MUST YOU DO IF THE ALARM "GAS" IS GIVEN?
A: Stop breathing.
   Put on your mask.
   Pass the word/sound the alarm.

12. Q: WHAT IS A BIOLOGICAL AGENT?
A: A living micro-organism which causes disease in man, animals, plants, and, to a lesser degree, deterioration of material.

13. Q: WHAT INFORMATION SHOULD YOU EXPECT TO FIND ON THE REAR OF A RADIOLOGICAL CONTAMINATION?
A: The dose rate.
   Date and time of dose rate reading.
   Date and time of the burst that produced the contamination (if known).

14. Q: WHAT DOES THE M13 KIT CONTAIN AND WHAT IS THE PURPOSE OF EACH ITEM?
A: A small pad filled with "Fuller's Earth" powder for absorbing chemical agents from the skin.
   Two cloth bags filled with a decontaminating and reimpregnation compound for detecting and eliminating the smear hazard of liquid contamination.
   A single-edge cutter to cut our spots of hazardous contamination on clothing.

**15. Q: WHAT INFORMATION WILL BE WRITTEN ON A BIOLOGICAL CON-

TAMINATION WARNING SIGN?
A: Name of the agent used.
   Date and time of detection.

16. Q: HOW IS NOTIFICATION OF THE TERMINATION OF A FALLOUT HAZARD CONDITION GIVEN?
A: Verbally, by the words "ALL CLEAR".

17. Q: HOW MAY PERSONNEL DECONTAMINATE THEMSELVES WHEN EXPOSED TO BIOLOGICAL AGENTS?
A: Shower with soap and hot water; germicidal soaps should be used, if available.

18. Q: WHAT ARE THE FIVE TYPES OF KNOWN ENEMY CHEMICAL AGENTS?
A: Nerve
   Blister
   Blood
   Choking
   Incapacitating

19. Q: HOW MAY A NERVE AGENT BE DISPERSED?
A: Aerosol
   Vapor
   Liquid droplet form

20. Q: WHAT ARE THE SYMPTOMS OF A NERVE AGENT ON MAN?
A: Difficult breathing
   Drooling
   Nausea
   Vomiting
   Convulsions
   Dim Vision (sometimes)

21. Q: WHAT ARE THE SYMPTOMS OF A BLISTER AGENT?
A: Searing of the eyes.
   Stinging of the skin.
   Irritation of the eyes and nose.

22. Q: WHAT ARE THE SYMPTOMS OF A BLOOD AGENT?
A: Convulsions
   Coma.

23. Q: WHAT THREE EFFECTS OF NUCLEAR WEAPONS PRODUCE CASUALTIES?
A: Blast
   Thermal radiation (heat and light)

Nuclear Radiation

24. Q: WHO IS RESPONSIBLE FOR INSPECTING, FITTING, ADJUSTING AND MAINTAINING A PROTECTIVE MASK?
A: The individual.

25. Q: GIVE AT LEAST THREE SITUATIONS WHEN THE FILTER ELEMENTS OF THE M17 MUST BE REPLACED?
A: When directed by the Commander or higher headquarters after prolonged usage.
At the first opportunity after exposure to one blood agent attack.
If they impose severe impedance to breathing, after immersion in water.
If on visual examination they are found to be damaged or unserviceable.
If the lot numbers do not match.

26. Q: WHAT SHOULD YOU DO WITH CONTAMINATED FILTER ELEMENTS FROM YOUR M17 AFTER THEY HAVE BEEN REPLACED?
A: Disposed of the filter elements by burying them under a few inches of soil.

27. Q: WHAT IS THE MAXIMUM NUMBER OF NERVE AGENT ANTIDOTE INJECTIONS AN INDIVIDUAL IS AUTHORIZED TO GIVE HIMSELF AND AT WHAT INTERVALS?
A: Three injections at 5/10 minute intervals.

28. Q: WHAT IS THE ALLOWABLE TIME FOR DONNING, SEATING CLEARING AND CHECKING YOUR PROTECTIVE MASK?
A: Nine seconds- with an additional six seconds to complete the attachment of the hood under the arms.

29. Q: DURING A NUCLEAR ATTACK THERE ARE THREE TYPES OF NUCLEAR RADIATION YOU WILL BE EXPOSED TO. WHAT ARE THEY?
A: Alpha rays.
Beta rays.
Gamma rays.

30. Q: WHAT DO THE LETTERS "NBC" STAND FOR?
A: Nuclear, Biological, Chemical.

31. Q: WHAT IS THE UNITED STATES POLICY ON THE USE OF BIOLOGICAL WEAPONS?
A: United States policy completely prohibits our use of biological weapons?

32. Q: WHAT IS THE U.S. POLICY ON THE USE OF CHEMICAL WEAPONS?
A: U.S. policy prohibits our using chemical weapons first.

33. Q: WHICH DETECTOR PAPER IS USED TO IDENTIFY CHEMICAL

AGENTS?
A: M8 Detection paper.

34. Q: WHAT ARE SOME OF THE EFFECTS OF NUCLEAR WEAPONS?
A: Blast, thermal radiation, and nuclear radiation.

35. Q: WHAT ARE THE EFFECTS OF BIOLOGICAL AGENTS?
A: They cause disease among personnel, animals, and plants.

36. Q: WHAT ARE THE THREE BASIC ROUTES WHICH BIOLOGICAL AGENTS MAY TAKE TO ENTER THE BODY?
A: Through the respiratory tract, a break in the skin, and through the digestive tract.

37. Q: WHAT ARE THE THREE TYPES OF NUCLEAR BURSTS?
A: Airburst, surface burst, and subsurface burst.

38. Q: WHAT ARE SOME OF THE PROBABLE ENEMY METHODS OF DELIVERING BIOLOGICAL AGENTS?
A: Aircraft spray, aerial bomblets, rockets, vectors, and sabotage.

39. Q: WHAT ARE THE FOUR TYPES OF CHEMICAL AGENTS?
A: Nerve agents, blister agents, blood agents, and choking agents.

40. Q: WHAT IS THE INDIVIDUAL FIRST AID FOR NERVE AGENTS?
A: Give Nerve Agent Antidote injections. Artificial respiration may be necessary.

41. Q: WHAT PROTECTIVE MEASURES SHOULD YOU TAKE IF YOU SUSPECT THAT THE ENEMY IS USING CHEMICAL AGENTS IN YOUR AREA OF OPERATIONS?
A: Stop breathing, mask, give the alarm, and continue the mission.

42. Q: WHAT IS THE MOST EFFECTIVE MEANS OF INFORMING TROOPS OF AN NBC HAZARD OR ATTACK?
A: The vocal alarm signal.

43. Q: WHAT IS THE VOCAL ALARM FOR ANY CHEMICAL ATTACK?
A: The word "GAS".

44. Q: WHAT MUST A SOLDIER DO BEFORE SHOUTING "GAS?"
A: Put on the protective mask.

45. Q: WHAT PROTECTIVE MASK IS NORMALLY ISSUED TO U.S. SOLDIERS?
A: The M-17 protective mask, however, this mask is being replaced on an attrition basis by the M-17A1 field protective mask.

46. Q: THE M-17 OR M-17A1 OFFERS NO PROTECTION AGAINST...?
A: Ammonia vapors or carbon monoxide.

47. Q: HOW LONG DO YOU HAVE TO PUT ON A PROTECTIVE MASK?
A: Nine seconds (15 seconds with the hood).

48. Q: WHAT PURIFIES THE AIR IN YOUR FIELD PROTECTIVE MASK?
A: Filter elements.

49. Q: WHAT ARE THE SYMPTOMS OF A CHEMICAL CASUALTY?
A: 1) A runny nose.
    2) A feeling of chocking and tightness in the chest or throat.
    3) Dimming of vision and difficulty in focusing the eyes on close objects.
    4) Irritations of the eyes.
    5) Difficulty in or increased rate of breathing.

50. Q: WHAT ARE THE SYMPTOMS OF NERVE GAS?
A: Nose starts running, chest feels tight, dimness of vision, twitching and breathing becomes difficult.

51. Q: WHAT SHOULD YOU DO IN CASE OF NERVE GAS EXPOSURE?
A: Mask, give the alarm, watch for signs of nerve agent poisoning and continue your mission.

52. Q: WHAT ARE THE SYMPTOMS OF A BLOOD AGENT?
A: Rapid breathing, rapid heart rate, headache, dizziness or gasping for air.

53. Q: WHAT SHOULD YOU DO IN CASE OF EXPOSURE TO A BLOOD AGENT?
A: Evacuate if possible.

54. Q: WHAT ARE THE SYMPTOMS OF A CHOKING AGENT?
A: Coughing, chocking, nausea, and headache.

55. Q: WHAT WOULD YOU DO IN CASE OF EXPOSURE TO A CHOCKING AGENT?
A: Avoid movement and keep warm.

56. Q: WHAT ARE THE SYMPTOMS OF BLISTER AGENTS?
A: Searing of the eyes and stinging of the skin.

57. Q: WHAT WOULD YOU DO IF YOU WERE EXPOSED TO A BLISTER AGENT?
A: Flush eyes with water and decontaminate your skin using the M258 kit.

58. Q: HOW CAN CASUALTIES FROM A BIOLOGICAL ATTACK BE RE-

DUCED?
A: Insure that your immunizations are up-to-date, place contaminated structures and areas under quarantine, practice rodent and pest control, know the proper care of cuts and wounds, and use only approved sources of food and drink.

59. Q: WHAT SHOULD YOU DO DURING AND AFTER A NUCLEAR ATTACK?
A: Stay calm, take cover and continue your mission.

60. Q: WHAT ARE THE SYMPTOMS OF RADIATION SICKNESS?
A: Vomiting, diarrhea, "dry heaving", nausea, lethargy, depression, and mental disorientation.

61. Q: WHICH TYPE OF NUCLEAR BURST CREATES THE MOST FALLOUT?
A: Surface.

62. Q: WHAT IS THE FIRST INDICATION OF A NUCLEAR EXPLOSION?
A: Intense light.

63. Q: WHAT ARE THE THREE CATEGORIES OF RADIATION?
A: Alpha, beta, and gamma.

64. Q: WHICH OF THE THREE TYPES OF RADIATION WILL AFFECT YOU THE MOST?
A: Gamma.

65. Q: WHAT COLOR ARE THE SIGNS FOR MARKING CONTAMINATED AREAS?
A: Gas- yellow triangle with red letters.
   Bio- blue triangle with red letters.
   Atom- white triangle with black letters.

66. Q: WHAT FORM DO CHEMICAL AGENTS COME IN?
A: Liquids, solids, and gases.

67. Q: NAME THREE METHODS USED TO DECONTAMINATE.
A: Flushing, neutralizing, destroying.

68. Q: WHAT IS THE SIGNAL FOR PROBABLE ATTACK BY AIRCRAFT OR MISSILES?
A: Steady siren blast of three minutes.

69. Q: WHAT IS THE SIGNAL FOR AN IMMINENT ENEMY ATTACK OR IF ONE IS TAKING PLACE?
A: A wailing or warbling siren blast of three minutes duration.

70. Q: WHAT IS THE ALL CLEAR SIGNAL?
A: Three each thirty second blasts separated by two thirty second silent periods.

71. Q: WHAT WOULD YOU DO IF YOU DISCOVERED THAT YOU HAVE A DROP OF NERVE AGENT ON YOUR SKIN?
A: Decontaminate the affected area using the M258 decon kit, and use the M13 decon kit on your clothing.

72. Q: UNDER WHAT CIRCUMSTANCES WOULD YOU MASK WITHOUT ORDERS?
A: Smoke from an unknown source is present, suspicious odors, liquid or solid is present. You are entering an area suspected of being contaminated. Your position is hit by smoke, mists, aerial spray, bombs, artillery or mortar fire.

73. Q: WHAT IS THE SELF AID/FIRST AID FOR WHITE PHOSPHOROUS?
A: Copper sulfate.

74. Q: IF YOU HAVE NO COPPER SULFATE, WHAT DO YOU USE FOR FIRST AID/SELF AID FOR WHITE PHOSPHOROUS?
A: Use anything that will smother the phosphorous. Mud is an excellent first aid/self aid until you can get medical help.

75. Q: WHAT IS THE SELF/FIRST AID FOR TEAR AGENTS?
A: Face into the wind, do not rub eyes.

76. Q: WHAT IS THE MAXIMUM NUMBER OF NERVE AGENT ANTIDOTE INJECTIONS CAN YOU GIVE FOR NERVE AGENTS?
A: Three.

77. Q: HOW LONG MUST A SOLDIER WAIT BEFORE GIVING HIMSELF THE SECOND INJECTION?
A: 5 - 10 minutes.

78. Q: WHAT ARE SOME OF THE WAYS WE MAY DETECT BIOLOGICAL AGENTS?
A: Sick plants, sick or dead animals or people, smoke or mist of an unknown nature without explanation.

79. Q: DESCRIBE SOME OF THE ACTIONS YOU WOULD TAKE IF YOU WERE UNDER ATOMIC ATTACK?
A: If forewarned, find a strong shelter, such as underground shelters, basements, deep foxholes, tanks, etc. If no time is available, lie flat in a ditch, low laying place in the ground or any shelter you can reach in a few steps and stay there until the heavy debris has stopped falling. Stay calm and try to reorganize your unit and be alert for orders and instructions. Expect an attack shortly

after the blast.

FM 22-5   **Drill and Ceremonies**

---

1. Q: WHAT ARE THE TWO PRESCRIBED FORMATIONS FOR A PLATOON?

A: Column and line.

2. Q: WHAT IS THE DIFFERENCE BETWEEN COLUMN AND LINE PLATOON FORMATIONS?
A: In a Column elements are one behind the other. In a Line the elements are abreast.

3. Q: WHAT IS CADENCE?
A: A uniform rhythm for moving troops.

4. Q: WHAT FIELD MANUAL GOVERNS DRILL AND CEREMONIES?
A: Field Manual (FM) 22-5.

5. Q: FOR CEREMONIAL FIRING, HOW MANY MEN ARE IN THE FIRING SQUAD?
A: Seven personnel and one noncommissioned officer.

6. Q: WHAT IS THE COMMAND GIVEN WHEN AN OFFICER ENTERS A MESS HALL DURING MEAL TIME?
A: At ease.

7. Q: WHAT ARE THE TWO PARTS OF A DRILL COMMAND?
A: Preparatory command and Command of execution.

8. Q: DEFINE THE FOLLOWING DRILL TERMS: RANK, FILE INTERVAL AND DISTANCE.
A: Rank- A single line of soldiers placed side by side.
    File- A single line of soldiers one behind the other.

Interval- Lateral space between elements.
Distance- Space between elements in a column.

9. Q: WHAT IS THE MAXIMUM NUMBER OF GUNS FIRED IN A NATIONAL SALUTE?
A: 21.

10. Q: WHAT IS THE OLDEST AND MOST COMMONLY USED DISPLAY OF MILITARY COURTESY?
A: The hand salute.

11. Q: WHAT IS MILITARY COURTESY?
A: It is the respect and consideration shown by the members of the military to each other.

12. Q: WHAT IS MEANT BY THE TERM "UNDER ARMS"?
A: It is carrying the Arms or having it attached to your person by sling or holster.

13. Q: WHO ENTERS A VEHICLE FIRST?
A: The junior soldier enters first and others follow in inverse order or rank.

14. Q: WHAT IS THE DIFFERENCE BETWEEN COLORS AND STANDARDS?
A: Colors- carried by dismounted troops.
   Standards- carried by mounted troops.

15. Q: WHAT IS THE CORRECT METHOD OF DISPOSING OF A WORN SILK NATIONAL COLOR?
A: It should be sent to the QM Corps for reconditioning. If the cost of reconditioning is found to be unwarranted, it will be returned to the unit for retention as a memento of service by the unit.

16. Q: WHERE IS THE FLAG FLOWN 24 HOURS A DAY?
A: The U.S. Capitol, Washington, D.C.
   Fort McHenry National Monument
   Historical Shrine, Flag House Square, Baltimore, MD.
   Francis Scott Key's Grave
   World War Memorial, Worcester MA
   USS Arizona, Pearl Harbor, HI
   Tomb of the Unknown Soldier
   The Moon

17. Q: WHEN THE NATIONAL FLAG BECOMES UNSERVICEABLE HOW SHALL IT BE DISPOSED OF?
A: According to an approved custom, the "stars" section is first cut from the flag and the two pieces which no longer form a flag are cremated. (NOTE: The

American flag is considered a living thing).

18. Q: WHAT IS MEANT BY NORMAL DISTANCE?
A: This is the space from the back of a soldier to the chest of the soldier immediately to his/her rear.

19. Q: WHAT IS THE ONLY POSITIONS FROM WHICH THE COMMAND "PARADE REST" MAY BE GIVEN?
A: The position of attention only.

20. Q: WHAT PROCEDURES WOULD YOU FOLLOW IF YOU WERE ON THE DRILL FIELD WITH A PLATOON OF SOLDIERS WHEN RETREAT IS SOUNDED?
A: Bring the platoon to attention.
  Face the platoon toward the flag (or music if the flag can not be seen).
  Give the command parade rest.
  After the cannon fires bring platoon to attention and present arms.

21. Q: WHAT IS A MUSTER FORMATION?
A: It is a company ceremonial formation to call the company roll to determine if all personnel are present.

22. Q: ASSUME YOU HAVE A PLATOON OF FOUR RANKS. YOU GIVE THE COMMAND "OPEN RANKS" - EXPLAIN WHAT EACH RANK MUST DO.
A: Front rank takes two steps forward.
  Second rank takes one step forward.
  Third rank stands fast.
  Fourth rank takes two steps backward.

23. Q: THERE ARE TWO SEPARATE COMMANDS WHICH MAY BE GIVEN TO CALL A FORMATION TO ATTENTION - WHAT ARE THEY?
A: Fall In and Attention.

24. Q: WHAT ORDER IS GIVEN IF YOU WISH TO CANCEL A PREPARATORY COMMAND?
A: As you were.

25. Q: AT THE COMMAND "PARADE REST" WHICH FOOT IS MOVED?
A: The left foot. Approximately 10 inches to the left of your right foot.

26. Q: WHEN MARCHING WHAT IS THE PROPER LENGTH STEP?
A: Thirty inches.

27. Q: IN A COLOR SQUAD, WHO CARRIES THE NATIONAL COLORS?
A: The ranking Noncommissioned Officer.

28. Q: WHAT ARE YOU ALLOWED TO DO WHEN GIVEN THE COMMAND

"AT EASE"?
A: You may move, keeping your right foot in place but you must remain silent.

29. Q: WHO MUST INITIATE A SALUTE?
A: The subordinate.

30. Q: WHAT IS A RETREAT FORMATION?
A: Retreat is a ceremony in which the unit plays honor to the United States flag when it is lowered in the evening.

31. Q: DURING "RETREAT", WHAT TWO MELODIES ARE PLAYED?
A: First "Retreat"
Secondly "To the Colors"

32. Q: WHO ORIGINATED DRILL AND WHEN?
A: Baron Von Steuben in 1788.

33. Q: WHEN DO YOU NOT RENDER A HAND SALUTE TO AN OFFICER?
A: When on a work detail, unless in charge.
When indoors, except when reporting to a commander.
When in formation, unless commanded to do so.

34. Q: THERE ARE THREE TYPES OF FLAGS. WHAT ARE THEY AND WHEN ARE THEY FLOWN?
A: Storm- Inclement weather.
Post- General display.
Garrison- Holidays and special occasions.

35. Q: HOW MANY STARS DOES OUR NATIONAL FLAG HAVE AND HOW ARE THEY ARRANGED?
A: There are 50 stars. Four rows of 5 and five rows of 6.

36. Q: CAN THE FLAG EVER BE FLOWN UPSIDE DOWN? IF SO, WHEN AND WHERE?
A: Yes. In time of distress, emergency, etc., at sea, during national emergencies at the Treasury Building in Washington D.C.

37. Q: WHEN EXECUTED FROM A HALT, ALL STEPS IN MARCHING BEGIN WITH THE LEFT FOOT EXCEPT ONE. NAME THE EXCEPTION.
A: Right step, march.

38. Q: WHAT IS THE CADENCE OF "QUICK TIME"?
A: Quick time is 120 steps per minute.

39. Q: WHAT IS THE CADENCE OF "DOUBLE TIME"?
A: Double time is 180 steps per minute.

40. Q: WHAT IS MEANT BY THE TERM "NORMAL INTERVAL"?
A: Right to left by the soldier on the right holding his left arm and hand shoulder high.

41. Q: WHEN WOULD AN ENLISTED SOLDIER NORMALLY SALUTE AN ENLISTED PERSON?
A: When reporting in a formation.
   When reporting for a board.

42. Q: WHAT IS THE CORRECT POSITION FOR A JUNIOR SOLDIER TO WALK IN RELATION TO A SOLDIER OF SENIOR GRADE?
A: The junior walks on the senior's left and one half pace behind.

43. Q: IF AN ENLISTED SOLDIER SALUTES AN OFFICER OUTSIDE AND GIVES HIM THE GREETING OF THE DAY, IS THE OFFICER REQUIRED BY REGULATION TO RETURN THE SALUTE?
A: Yes.

44. Q: WHEN YOU ARE DISPLAYING ANOTHER FLAG WITH THE NATIONAL FLAG, HOW SHOULD THE NATIONAL FLAG BE DISPLAYED?
A: To the right and higher. As you face them, the national flag would appear to the left.

45. Q: WHAT IS ALIGNMENT?
A: The arrangement of several elements on the same line.

46. Q: MOST COMMANDS HAVE TWO PARTS, WHAT ARE THEY?
A: Preparatory command and command of execution.

47. Q: WHAT COMMAND IS GIVEN IN ASSUMING THE POSITION OF ATTENTION?
A: Fall in or squad/platoon attention.

48. Q: THE HAND SALUTE IS A HOW MANY COUNT MOVEMENT?
A: One count movement.

49. Q: WHAT FORMATION IS THE SQUAD NORMALLY FOUND IN?
A: Line formation.

50. Q: THE SQUAD IS DISMISSED ONLY FROM WHAT FORMATION?
A: Line formation.

51. Q: TO FORM A COLUMN FROM A LINE FORMATION, WHAT COMMAND IS GIVEN?
A: Right, face.

**52. Q: TO MARCH IN THE OPPOSITE DIRECTION, WHAT COMMAND IS

GIVEN?
A: Rear march.

53. Q: WHAT IS NORMAL INTERVAL?
A: The lateral space between soldiers measured from right to left by the person on the right holding their left arm up shoulder high, fingers and thumb extended and joined with the top of the middle finger touching the right shoulder of the person next to him.

54. Q: IN DRILL AND CEREMONIES, WHAT DOES THE FOLLOWING TERM MEAN: RANK?
A: A rank is a line which is only one element in depth.

55. Q: WHAT IS HEAD?
A: A head is the leading element of a column.

56. Q: WHAT IS A FLANK?
A: Flank is the right or left side of any formation as sensed by an element within that formation.

57. Q: WHAT IS A FILE?
A: A file is a column which has a front of only one element.

58. Q: WHAT IS A FRONT?
A: Front is the space from side to side of a formation including the right and left element.

59. Q: WHAT IS DEPTH?
A: The space from front to rear of a formation including the front and rear elements.

60. Q: WHAT ARE CEREMONIES?
A: Ceremonies are formations and movements in which a number of troops execute movement in unison with a precision just as in drill.

61. Q: WHAT DOES DRILL MEAN?
A: Drill consists of certain movements by which a unit or individuals are moved in an orderly, uniform manner from one formation to another, or from one place to another.

62. Q: WHAT ARE SUPPLEMENTARY COMMANDS?
A: Oral orders given by a subordinate leader that reinforce and complement a commander's order which insures proper understanding and execution of a movement.

63. Q: WHAT IS INFLECTION?
A: Inflection is the rise and fall in pitch and the tone change of the voice.

64. Q: WHAT IS CADENCE?
A: Cadence, in commands, means the uniform and rhythmic flow of words.

65. Q: ALL MARCHING MOVEMENTS EXECUTED FROM THE HALT ARE INITIATED FROM WHAT POSITION?
A: Attention.

66. Q: WHEN EXECUTED FROM THE HALT ALL STEPS EXCEPT WHAT BEGIN WITH THE LEFT FOOT?
A: Right step.

67. Q: TO CHANGE STEP WHILE MARCHING THE COMMAND CHANGE STEP IS GIVEN AS WHAT FOOT STRIKES THE GROUND?
A: Right foot.

68. Q: TO MARCH WITH A 15 INCH STEP FROM THE HALT WHAT COMMAND IS GIVEN?
A: Half step march.

69. Q: WHAT ARE THE LENGTHS OF THE FOLLOWING STEPS?
A: Quick time- 30 inches.
   Double time- 30 inches.
   Backward step- 15 inches.
   Half step- 15 inches.

70. Q: WHAT ARE THE TWO RECOMMENDED FORMATIONS FOR CONDUCTION REVIEWS?
A: Battalion or Brigade in line.

71. Q: DO THE NATIONAL COLORS RENDER SALUTES?
A: No.

72. Q: WHAT IS REVEILLE?
A: A ceremony in which the unit honors the national flag as it is raised in the morning.

73. Q: WHAT IS RETREAT?
A: A ceremony in which the unit pays honor to the national flag when it is lowered in the evening.

74. Q: WHAT IS COMMAND RETREAT?
A: A retreat ceremony conducted with all members of the command present.

75. Q: WHAT ARE THE THREE CLASSES OF MILITARY FUNERALS?
A: With chapel service, without chapel service, with grave side services only.

76. Q: FOR CEREMONIAL FIRING WHAT IS THE MAXIMUM NUMBER OF RIFLEMEN AND NCO'S?
A: No more than seven riflemen and one NCO.

77. Q: WHAT IS A GUIDON?
A: The guidon is a company, battery, or troop identification flag.

78. Q: WHAT DOES STEP MEAN?
A: The prescribed distance measured from heel to heel of a marching soldier.

OTHER TITLES

Mr. Spear's training manuals are highly regarded by the professionals and the national magazines. John Coleman, editor of **Soldier of Fortune Magazine**, says, *"These are not re-hashes of armchair-warrior theory; Spear has a hands-on knowledge stemming from years spent as a military trainer around the world, and the singular ability to express it in writing. Well worth a phone call or letter— it might just keep you alive down the road."*

Denny Hansen, editor of **SWAT Magazine**, says, *"Spear's ability to use simple, concise language when he teaches makes it easy for a novice to understand while adding to the expert's knowledge base as well."*

You may want to order three other closely related Spear titles to complete your reference library. Each is designed for specific, differing applications, so they tend to complement one another. Taken as a whole, they comprise one of the most complete and versatile fighting systems and security program guidelines available on the market today. Use the order blank on the last page.

Survival On The Battlefield: A Handbook To Military Martial Arts
$14.95 ISBN: 0-86568-093-0
8.5 x 11 Trade Paperback
190 pages, 350 photos

A training course in military martial arts designed for killing and maiming. Techniques from ten different systems were selected for ease of learning and effective execution. Much information for unit trainer's programs. Has been used by the 3rd Special Forces Group.

Close-Quarters Combat For Police And Security Forces
$19.95 ISBN: 0-9622627-4-9
8.5 x 11 Trade Paperback
128 pages, 350 photos

Using a similar format to the military book, these methods, however, focus around controling and containment plus nightstick techniques. This manual also provides much assistance to the unit trainer as well as the student.

Surviving Hostage Situations
with Special Operations Officer, Major D. Michael Moak
$14.95 ISBN: 0-9622627-5-7
8.5 x 11 Trade Paperback
144 pages, 60 illustrations

Written for the layman and families, this manual provides sound advice on how to make it through criminal, terrorist, and prison hostage situations. Now used as a manual for volunteer workers at the Kansas State Penitentiary. Professionals love its down to earth style and the fill-in-the-blanks contingency plan provided as an appendix.

Spear's training style is consistent and easy to understand. His unique training philosophies weave their way through these manuals like ribbons of light. If you liked **Military Knife Fighting**, you'll love the rest of this series. Order them today!

ORDER FORM

UNIVERSAL FORCE DYNAMICS
410 DELAWARE
LEAVENWORTH, KS 66048
(913) 682-6518

Title	QTY	Price	Total
Military Knife Fighting		$ 9.95	
Survival on the Battlefield		$14.95	
Close-Quarters Combat for Police		$19.95	
Surviving Hostage Situations		$14.95	
		Subtotal	
5.25% Sales Tax (Kansas Residents)			
		Shipping & Handling	$3.00
		Total Cost	

Name _____
Address _____
City / State _____
ZIP _____